ADVANCE PRAISE FOR
THE HOMEBREWER'S ALMANAC

"It's amazing how quickly 'The Scratch Way' has come to mean a particular—and natural—way of brewing for a growing number of beer fans. *The Homebrewer's Almanac* is a perfect introduction into brewing for experienced foragers and an equally delightful introduction into foraging for experienced brewers."

—Stan Hieronymus, author of *Brew Like a Monk* and *Brewing Local*

"While the folks at Scratch Brewing did not invent the concept of brewing with 'alternative' ingredients, they have elevated botanical and foraged beers to a level that commands deserved respect amongst the ranks of craft brewers. Just like their beers, *The Homebrewer's Almanac* represents an artful, creative presentation that allows the ingredients to speak for themselves. This one-of-a-kind book is a worthy addition to any brewer's collection."

—Matthew McCarroll, PhD, Professor of Chemistry and Biochemistry
and Director of the Fermentation Science Institute,
Southern Illinois University Carbondale

"*The Homebrewer's Almanac* is the most meaningful and significant statement made to date in the movement toward creating beer that's inextricably linked to a place and time. In an age where technological advances have made it possible to brew the same beer virtually anywhere on Earth, the knowledge and practical wisdom that Josephson, Kleidon, and Tockstein have amassed is critical to restoring the important connection between beer and our own immediate surroundings."

—Jeffrey Stuffings, founder of Jester King Brewery

THE
HOMEBREWER'S
ALMANAC

THE HOMEBREWER'S ALMANAC

A SEASONAL GUIDE TO MAKING YOUR OWN BEER FROM SCRATCH

Marika Josephson, Aaron Kleidon, and Ryan Tockstein

Photographs by Aaron Kleidon

The Countryman Press
A division of W. W. Norton & Company
Independent Publishers Since 1923

For information about permission to reproduce selections from this book, write to Permissions, The Countryman Press, 500 Fifth Avenue, New York, NY 10110

For information about special discounts for bulk purchases, please contact W. W. Norton Special Sales at specialsales@wwnorton.com or 800-233-4830

Manufacturing through Asia Pacific Offset
Book design by Endpaper Studio

Library of Congress Cataloging-in-Publication Data

Names: Josephson, Marika, author. | Kleidon, Aaron, author. | Tockstein,
   Ryan, author.
Title: The homebrewer's almanac : a seasonal guide to making your own beer
   from scratch / Marika Josephson, Aaron Kleidon, and Ryan Tockstein.
Description: New York : The Countryman Press, a division of W. W. Norton &
   Company, [2016] | Includes index.
Identifiers: LCCN 2016017587 | ISBN 9781581573497 (pbk.)
Subjects: LCSH: Beer. | Brewing—Amateurs' manual.
Classification: LCC TP577 .J67 2016 | DDC 663/.3—dc23
LC record available at https://lccn.loc.gov/2016017587

The Countryman Press
www.countrymanpress.com

A division of W. W. Norton & Company
500 Fifth Avenue, New York, NY 10110
www.wwnorton.com

10 9 8 7 6 5 4 3 2

To everyone in our community who has helped us create these beers and this place

CONTENTS

PREFACE

The woods enchant us: every pine sapling with its outsized needles, every fallen oak tree and its mushroom denizens, every bitter green leaf and tannic root, every paw paw hidden beneath the fall leaves. The three of us spend a lot of time in the woods—not just to make beer, but because the woods speak to us. We take its pulse; we respect its force. It has a special language we sometimes hear and more rarely speak.

Brewing an elixir with leaves, bark, nuts, and roots from familiar trees, each with its own story, is incantatory. The adventure offered by following the guidance of medicine men and women, ancient homebrewers, and our farming ancestors—all the while taking divergent paths to find surprising new flavors—is the intoxicating heart of why we make beer. Many of the plants from which we harvest have been in the woods longer than we have been alive, and will be here well after we've gone. Carrying on the heritage of ancient traditions brings us closer to the long life cycle of the plants we briefly live with side-by-side.

The techniques in this book have been developed over the last five or six years that we've been brewing together. They are a time-stamp of our current understanding of several dozen plants after hundreds of brews and experiments. In the recipes included here you will find information about how people have traditionally used those plants and how we've experimented with them, as well as tips on harvesting and preserving. In some cases we mention edible parts of plants we have yet to brew with ourselves. We hope that after understanding the techniques in this book you can try some of those suggestions at home. We also hope that you will use those techniques on the plants, trees, leaves, herbs, roots, and fruit that we don't mention in this book but that exist in your part of the world.

We brew with what we have around us. We make beers that taste and smell like this place. We don't order fruit extracts to make fruit beers; we use persimmons, apples, peaches, elderberries, and other whole fruits from our woods and fields. We do this in part because of the high quality of these ingredients and the ease of harvesting them only miles (sometimes yards) from our brewing stand, and in part as a statement about industrial agriculture. We support our local farmers and our local food systems. We make small-scale beer that supports tight-knit communities.

We hope that after reading this book you will start to take the pulse of the life around you and bring it into your brewing process. Perhaps in so doing you will feel more connected to the incredible diversity of nature that exists—often precariously—all around us.

We hope the woods will enchant you.

INTRODUCTION

Just as cooking with fresh seasonal produce enhances the flavors in food, the same is true of beer. Freshly harvested plants, from peaches to pecans, are leaps and bounds more flavorful and aromatic than most internationally sourced supermarket-bought produce, since very often those plants are bred for long voyages and picked before they've fully developed. To put it in beer terms, would you prefer to brew a beer with a hop that was picked before it was ready and shipped under unknown temperature conditions for an unspecified period of time, or with a hop freshly picked off the bine from somewhere near your home? Flavor and aroma in any plant works exactly the same way it does in hops; picking, shipping, and seasonality will dramatically affect the quality of the beer you make.

Chances are, most people reading this book have access to freshly picked ingredients from gardens or regional farms, even if they live in the middle of a big urban center. We are lucky to be living in a time in which people are finding their way back to the land—even if the land is stacked on a wall or planted on a rooftop garden—and farmers' markets are proliferating. Nearly everyone is a walk, bus ride, car trip, or train stop from fresh, seasonal produce.

Farmed plants are familiar to most people, but the idea of foraging may feel somewhat more foreign, particularly for anyone living in a city or suburb. Where do you start with foraging if you've never done it before? How do you know what's safe and what's toxic? How do you identify plants that look similar but have different, possibly poisonous effects? We have included a variety of foraged plants in this book, from the simplest and most easily identifiable to those that are slightly more difficult to identify and procure. A dandelion is a dandelion whether it grows in your front yard or in a field. You may not have thought twice about the juniper on your block in Phoenix, or the lavender that lines your sidewalk in Seattle, but they grow ubiquitously in many cities and suburbs, are easy to identify, and can all be used in beer.

We are located in the Midwest, so the ingredients in our recipes are biased toward this region; however, our home base of southern Illinois is a large area, almost equal in size to Connecticut, and lies between the Mississippi and the Ohio Rivers with Kentucky, Indiana, and Missouri on its borders—nestled between the heartland and the south. Its temperature and location make it one of the richest places for flora in the country, with biomes that overlap with many other parts of the United States. Some of the many communities that provide plant diversity here include moist ravines, ditches, swamps, marshes, stream beds, sandy river banks, hill prairies, rocky slopes, and sandstone and limestone ledges, springs, and caves.

Hopefully, this book will help all you homebrewers take advantage of the diverse plants in your region. Once you learn what is possible with leaves, roots, bark, seeds, flowers, or fruit, the possibilities for applying our techniques to local plants—wherever you are—is endless.

SIMPLE TIPS FOR FARMING AND FORAGING

Before going into detail about technique, there are half a dozen simple things you can do to make better beer with plants. Here are a few hints about selecting cultivated ingredients and beginning to forage.

Choose Heirloom Plants

Many plants have been cultivated over the years for a longer shelf life at the expense of flavor. Heirloom varieties are the opposite. They are plants that were cultivated before the advent of hybridized mass farming. Seeds of these varieties will prove "true to type" when planted, and therefore carry the same color, flavor, and aroma profiles as their forebears. Some varieties are centuries old with fantastic stories as rich as any history book, and have stronger, more distinct flavor profiles. They may not taste exactly what you think a certain plant *should* taste like, but invariably they will have a profoundly more robust flavor that can be used to greater effect. For instance, we have grown an heirloom Wapsipinicon peach tomato that—almost unbelievably—feels fuzzy like a peach, is fleshy and orange on the inside like a peach, and, well, tastes a whole lot like a peach. However, the peach flavor has the added acidity and earthiness of the tomato that makes a great addition to a saison or a Belgian single. There are thousands of heirloom varieties of plants, each one with its unique imprint, offering endless flavor combinations for beer.

Join a CSA

To access fresh and flavorful plants, we also recommend joining a CSA. That's shorthand for Community Supported Agriculture. Through CSAs, farms across the country offer shares that allow people to pay up-front and receive a weekly or semi-weekly delivery of a bounty of seasonal produce, even in the heart of a big city. Most of the time you can't choose exactly what you will get, but the trade-off is that everything you do get is the freshest and highest quality produce available. This book in many ways is made for the person who belongs to a CSA and receives a bounty of 20 pounds of squash—but has no idea what to do with the 15 pounds left over after three weeks of soup has been made. And while squash and pumpkin beers may be more common these days, the truth is you can brew with almost anything! Leftover fennel bulbs? Put them in a Belgian stout. Too many parsnips? Add them to a smoky black ale.

Plant an Herb Garden

We can't sing high enough praises for the seasonal herb garden. Anyone, anywhere can grow herbs. They are the magical ingredients that breathe life into the simplest foods, and can add dramatic panache to your beer. Best of all, you can pick them moments before putting them into your boil, ensuring the greatest aromatic possibilities. We make a beer entirely with herbs from our garden (no hops)—just a handful of five or six varieties that are available when we brew, usually lavender, basil, rosemary, sage, mint, and lemon thyme. The result is a complex mix of flavors that morphs with each sip and even evolves over time—a great beer to age and experience as it develops. A windowsill herb garden is more than enough to add a little extra character to your beer.

Learn About Wild Plants

So much for tame plants, what about wild plants?

People who are just getting into foraging for the first time have asked us for tips about identifying plants or learning how to forage. We should note that this book is not an identification guide and shouldn't be used for that purpose. Dr. John Kallas's *Edible Wild Plants: Wild Foods from Dirt to Plate* is a very good guide, as is Samuel Thayer's *Nature's Garden*. Both have clear photographs and extensive information. *Stalking the Wild Asparagus* by Euell Gibbons is a classic text still in print, as is the slightly more recent *Edible Wild Plants: A North American Field Guide* by Thomas Elias and Peter Dykeman. There should also be regional guides to edible plants in your area. A reliable one is the Peterson Guide. It's helpful to have several guides with pictures and descriptions to give you the most information possible. Just remember that there is no truly authoritative book on foraging; foraging is a lifetime practice. A collection of books will prove more valuable, especially for beginners.

In addition, there are a handful of great

WHY BUY LOCAL FOOD?

Simply put, it is a matter of health. For Plato, the health of the state hinged on each person doing what was in their nature and not overstepping their bounds. Farmers, for whom the cultivation of crops was essential to their being, were foundational because they grew food for the citizens of the republic; in fact they are the first type of citizens Plato names as fundamental members of a city, because nutrition (in the sense of feeding and being fed, and in the sense of health) is vital.

But farmers don't just tend crops, they take care of the soil—both as a matter of health and to preserve their way of life. Farmers are not only one link in the chain of a community, they are one link in a chain of nature; they are the interlocutors between nature and society. When we maintain mineral-rich soil, we preserve the land with which we have been entrusted, and we pass mineral-rich produce on to individuals. The health of the soil is transferred to plants, animals, individuals, families, rural communities, cities, cultures, societies, and the economy. Farmland that prospers leads to cities that flourish; and cities that flourish do so by supporting the health of the land.

Our republic is made of small rural communities and ever larger cities, which have become more and more detached from the everyday lives of farms, farmers, and the soil. We have seen a steady drain of younger generations out of rural communities and into urban areas, while at the same time we have concentrated farming into regions that have perhaps overstepped the bounds within which farmers can functionally grow our food as a nation. Crop diversity in the heartland has been reduced to soybeans, corn, and wheat; California and Mexico grow the rest of our produce and ship unripe, nutrient-poor food throughout this massive country. Our health as a republic suffers. And if farming conditions fail in one region where most of our food is grown, we suffer again.

Farming, like so many other trades, is best learned in the field—hands in the soil, under the sun and rain. It is a trade that is learned as a community. We prosper with our farmers and we do best when supporting regional communities as part of a dynamic chain from the soil and back again.

ON FORAGING

Foraging is a result of knowledge, understanding, and awareness gained over time. These three components are so interrelated that where one stops and another begins is blurry. All plants and their environments are pieces of a whole. One cannot exist without the others.

Becoming aware of what's around you is the first step in learning any trade, including foraging. But nature exists outside of human practice. Its processes occur whether they are seen or heard by people. Foraging is therefore about tuning our senses to our environment. As we become comfortable and relaxed in a place, we begin to notice things. These things can be as simple as noticing what month a plant emerges from the soil, or as complex as recognizing when a bird or other animal begins to gather seed from a certain stalk.

Knowledge like this takes practice, and to practice one must spend time in a place; to learn about the forest, go to the forest. The same applies to the prairie, the mountains, or the desert. Take notes, read field guides, listen, smell—but most importantly, enjoy. It can be overwhelming looking at all the plants in one square meter of land, let alone the entire forest or field, but relaxing your mind in the space you are learning will give you what you need to know eventually. Look at the leaves and bark on trees. At first they appear similar, but over time they will start to differentiate themselves, and eventually these distinctions will become obvious.

It's also important to spend time in a place over the course of the seasons. A plant cannot be harvested in winter if we have not seen it throughout the year. What color was the flower, the shape of the stem, the seeds, the leaves? Is it a perennial? One cannot understand one season completely without understanding the other three; it's just as important to be in the forest in the winter as it is to explore it in the summer. And different plants have different relationships to a myriad of factors like weather, sunlight exposure, soil types, and other plants, animals, and people. All these things take time to learn and understand. Even after years in the same space, you notice new connections. But once you start to understand these relationships, finding and harvesting plants becomes much easier.

It's scary to think that some people view gathering plants from the wild as a fad. Nature can grow plants far better than we as humans can. Gathering plants from the wild has been important to all cultures; why should ours be any different? Foraging is the product of time. It is something that cannot be learned quickly or all at once. It cannot ever be fully understood—but that's what makes it mysterious and exciting. In the vein of Wes Jackson, wild spaces hold the answers to questions we have yet to ask!

encyclopedias of plants that describe planting, harvesting, traditional uses by many peoples, health, toxicity, and medicinal aspects. One classic text is *A Modern Herbal* by Maude Grieve. We consult a number of other guides on a weekly basis, including a handful of books that describe how to use plants for brewing. A list of texts we recommend is included at the end of the book.

Find an Expert

The best way to learn about plants is with an expert who knows the plants in your area. If you don't know anyone, start by visiting your local farmers' market and seeing what people have to offer there—often there are people selling foraged ingredients who are bursting with information and may be happy to take you on a walk. Most regions also have parks, botanical gardens, or similar spaces with educated guides and nature walks. Generally, getting out and meeting people involved in nature, plants, or farming will lead you in the right direction. Starting with easy plants like dandelion or honeysuckle will also help you learn about identification and build confidence as you get deeper into the world of foraging and learn about other plants in your area. Some of these easily recognizable plants may be weeds, but what is a weed, really? Sometimes it's just a plant whose name is unknown. Once you learn the name, research the plant and learn how it's used by people who are from the area.

THE BREWING PROCESS

Many readers are probably already familiar with brewing. If so, skip this part and go ahead to the next section, which has general tips on how to integrate plants into your beer.

For those who have only a passing acquaintance—or no acquaintance at all—with brewing, here is a short introduction. In our Resources page at the end of the book we include suggestions for books that will help you go more in depth.

Truth is, brewing can be as simple or as complex as you want to make it. Your basic ingredients are malted grains (barley, wheat, rye, even spelt or quinoa), water, yeast, hops, and other flavoring ingredients like the plants in this book. The simplest equipment can be a kettle for boiling, a plastic bucket or carboy with an airlock for fermentation, some hoses for transferring liquid, and a thermometer—plus bottles, bottle caps, and a bottle capper to package your finished product. Since everything that touches the beer after the end of the boil must be perfectly clean and sanitized, you will need some kind of sanitizing product to rinse your fermentation vessels, and to soak the hoses and bottles.

Extract brewing is the easiest way to begin. In this method, you buy syrup already made from malted grains, and dissolve it into water in a kettle. As your water comes up to the right temperature, you can steep other specialty grains—like roasted barley for stouts or crystal malts for toast or caramel flavor—to add complexity. After removing those grains, boil the malt liquid (known as wort) with hops or other flavoring agents. Then cool to about room temperature, add your yeast, and let it go to town. Yeast eats sugar, and the byproducts of its digestive process are alcohol and carbon dioxide, which is how you get alcohol and bubbles in your finished product.

All-grain brewing is a bit more complex. In this method you extract the sugars from the grains yourself, adding water to the grains at a specific temperature for about an hour, then transferring the sugary liquid to the kettle to boil. This requires another vessel in which you can mash your grains, and that vessel can be as fancy as you want to make it. Many people use a converted water cooler, as the insulation in the cooler helps keep the mash at a specific temperature. You can buy converted coolers from home brew shops, or there are many places to find instructions for building one yourself with simple parts you can purchase at a construction supply store. But you can use any container you can dream of, as long as it is big enough to hold your water and grains; includes some kind of false bottom to separate the grains and allow the malt liquid to run through, plus a spout to drain the liquid; and has a fairly strong layer of insulation to hold the temperature. After mashing your grains and running the liquid into the kettle, the rest of the process is the same as in extract brewing. All of the recipes in this book are geared toward all-grain brewing. You can find conversions for all of the recipes for extract brewing on page 195.

Most boil times are 60 to 90 minutes. The process of boiling adds some kettle caramelization for flavor while extracting bitterness, flavor, and aroma from hops or other plants, and can also get rid of unwanted off-flavors from certain grains. When boiling is complete, you will need to chill the wort down to about room temperature (anywhere between 66 and 72 degrees, roughly) quickly to pitch your yeast. You can do this very simply by setting up an ice water bath in a large sink or bathtub. Unfortunately, this method can take a lot of time, which may allow off-flavors to develop or possibly infect the wort with bacteria. An alternative is to make a small investment in a stainless-steel or copper-coiled wort chiller, which goes directly into the kettle and sends cold water around in a loop to chill the wort.

Fermentation usually takes one to two weeks, or sometimes a little longer depending on the beer. Airlocks are a good indication of when fermentation is complete. They bubble as carbon dioxide is released while the yeast is active, and stop when the yeast has finished eating sugars. An inexpensive investment that will give you a much clearer picture of your fermentation is a hydrometer. Hydrometers measure the amount of sugar in a solution; you will see a decrease in sugar as fermentation comes to completion, and finally no change when fermentation is complete. Since you know that the sugar consumed has been turned into alcohol in the process, taking one reading at the beginning of fermentation (called the original gravity, or OG) and one at the end (called the final gravity, or FG) allows you to do a simple mathematical conversion to give you the alcohol content of your finished product.

At the end of fermentation you have two different ways to package your beer. The simplest way is to transfer your beer into a sanitized bucket, add priming sugar, and run the beer into bottles. The added sugar will reinvigorate the yeast so that it naturally carbonates the beer in the bottle. You can use empty beer bottles you've collected or buy new ones. Remember that everything that touches your beer after the end of the boil must be completely sanitized. A dishwasher with the heat cycle is an easy way to go even further and sterilize bottles. But just dunking the bottles and caps in sanitizer for 20 seconds will do the trick. A cheap double-lever bottle capper works well to press the crown caps onto the tops of the bottles.

BREWING WITH PLANTS

Brewing with something other than malt, hops, water, or yeast will inject an X factor into your plans. Since these four ingredients have been the basis of beer since roughly the Middle Ages, they have been subjected to the greatest amount of study and scrutiny. It's incredible to think that we can take any hop off of a bine, any yeast from cold storage, any grain from a malting floor, any drop of water from a faucet, and calculate their bittering, flavoring, and attenuation potentials. As modern brewers, we can take a scientific approach to brewing, and this has undoubtedly led to some of the greatest advancements in brewing techniques and the extremely high quality beer we enjoy today. However, this method can often instill anxiety any time we encounter unknown variables.

Every plant in this book is a variable. Scientists haven't measured the bittering potential of dandelions; you won't know the chemistry of maple sap on your brew day. However, this is no cause for trepidation! We're embarking on a journey that will bring a world of flavors and aromas beyond the tried and true malt, hop, water, yeast combination we know so well. It's 1492 and we're sending Christopher Columbus out to traverse the open ocean. He knows nothing of the Reinheitsgebot. A little bit of adventure and the spirit of improvisation will serve us well in this endeavor.

Tips for Experimentation

We're a small-batch brewery. Full batches of our beer would be considered a "pilot" batch for many other breweries. But we also started as homebrewers, and we learned a lot from "small" homebrew batches. Experimentation often happens with a scaled down version of a bigger idea.

As a home brewer you might consider breaking your 5-gallon batches into five 1-gallon batches, or two 2½-gallon batches. Use the small batches to boil with different plants, and see how each plant changes the final product. Decide which version you like best, then scale up.

One technique we use often with an ingredient we've never tried in a beer is to make a tea with it. Teas simulate the act of boiling or steeping, and we can learn a lot about bitterness and aroma before we take the step to mash our grains and ferment. Teas also help us decide what malts will complement the bitterness and flavor of the plants, and which yeast will bring out other flavors and aromas. On a typical day at Scratch, Aaron will walk into the kitchen with a handful of roots or a new flower he's identified. We'll make a tea, pass it around, and brainstorm beer styles, malt profiles, and yeast characteristics that would combine to create an interesting beer with what we're smelling and tasting.

Probably the most important thing to remember as you get into the spirit of experimentation is to let your guard down and to have an open mind. These are new flavors and new ingredients. They're not going to taste exactly like the beer you're used to, and that's a good thing. Don't worry too much about exact measurements, and don't be afraid of a little dirt. If you follow the basic rules of sanitation your beer will turn out fine even if a mushroom has a little soil under its gills. Our dos and don'ts list is pretty short, but it will always produce palatable beer:

DO care about sanitation and fermentation temperature.

DON'T care about calculating IBUs.

Everything else can be approximated.

This may sound nerve-wracking, but it's also freeing to just let the beer be what it will be. If your mind is open to the idea that these beers are going to smell and taste a little out of the ordinary, you'll be able to appreciate a whole new drinking and brewing experience.

General Techniques for Brewing with Plants

We've developed a number of general techniques for brewing with a variety of plants and parts of plants, which we outline below. Some of these methods are based on historical brewing styles. Others are based on how plants were used as medicine in traditional cultures. Other methods we developed out of fermentation and infusion techniques found in wine-making or the distillation of spirits. Still others we discovered after random accidents we encountered while experimenting with (or forgetting about!) something in our brewhouse. Use these techniques as guidelines for your own experimentation and consider them jumping-off points for developing techniques of your own.

Roots

Let's start from the ground and work our way up, beginning with what lies underground: roots. Roots come in all shapes and sizes, and chances are you've already used or thought about using a few familiar examples like ginger or sweet potato. But there are other roots that you may not have even thought about. Dandelion root, for instance, was once used as a coffee substitute, as was chicory root—which you can still find blended into coffee at a few places like Café du Monde in New Orleans. Other roots were boiled or steeped as teas and used for medicinal purposes in traditional Native American cultures, as well as by colonial-era Americans.

Ginger and roots like it are a great place to start. Think about the spicy character they lend to any dish, or to drinks like ginger ale or ginger beer. Ginger and similar roots like turmeric or goldenseal are best utilized as a flavoring addition because of the pungent spiciness they add. In our experience, roots like these lose nothing from a long boil, and can be roughly chopped to make a little go a long way. Like hot peppers, you should experiment with these roots by starting small and adding more to subsequent batches until you achieve the flavor balance you prefer. Try a pound of ginger or turmeric in a 5-gallon batch and see how you like the results. (And if you find that it's too much for your taste, let the beer condition for a while before serving. The flavor will die back over time.) In contrast, goldenseal is extremely powerful and several grams may be more than enough for your beer. Make a tea first with any root to see how bitter and aromatic it will be.

Some roots, like dandelion and arugula, are better for bittering. The root, like the green part of the plant, is bitter and can take the place of a low alpha acid hop for low- to moderately-hopped beers. You can also roast bitter roots until nearly black and grind them up as you would to make coffee—this is how dandelion would traditionally have been

made into a coffee substitute. Do this to add extra coffee-like roastiness with a hint of earth and bitterness to any beer, particularly stouts or porters. You can add the grinds straight to the boil, or to the fermenter after primary fermentation, or you can make a "coffee" infusion and add the liquid to the

fermenter. We usually roast at 350 degrees Fahrenheit until the root is chocolate brown to black.

Tubers offer a different way of looking at roots. These are roots that we often eat for their starch content, and the starches can be converted into sugars by mashing and using as an alternative fermentable. Potato and sweet potato are two of the most obvious tubers, and looking farther south, we can find possibilities in manioc and cassava.

In addition, the sugary starches can be caramelized and added to the beer in a totally different way. Imagine sweet potato pie, or the way that potatoes will caramelize when roasted in foil over a hot fire on the grill. We very often roast starchy roots like sweet potatoes and other sugary gourds to bring out the natural sugars, allowing them to caramelize. This will add an extra hint of burnt sugar and caramel to the beer. Try roasting in an oven at

400 degrees Fahrenheit, the way you might make butternut squash soup. Once the tuber or gourd is starting to caramelize, add it to the fermenter.

Mushrooms

Dancing around many roots and on the sides of trees throughout the year are fungi of all shapes and colors. Unless you've grown up in or around the woods, you may be most familiar with grocery store varieties of mushrooms. However, it's becoming more commonplace to see dried varieties of very flavorful mushrooms like chanterelle and porcini, as well as cultivated mushrooms like oyster, shiitake, and even hen of the woods, popping up in supermarket aisles. We've played around with lots of mushrooms in beer, and yet there still seems to be a lot to learn about how best to infuse their unique flavors. Chanterelles and black trumpet mushrooms, which are related, are some of the most flavorful fungi, and we've had good results adding them to the end of the boil after drying them first to concentrate their flavors. Some mushrooms like turkey tail are often dried and added to soup stocks, increasing the earthy umami flavor of the soup. Overall, this is a very effective technique for beer. If you can rehydrate the mushrooms first in hot water, then let them steep for 24 hours, you'll be able to get more flavor than you would by steeping at room temperature.

But other mushrooms have proved more elusive. Hen-of-the-woods mushrooms, for instance, have a coconut-like aroma that hits you over the head in the boil, but seems to become lost after fermentation. We haven't yet discovered the ideal way to add these to a beer. An alcoholic tincture may work. Perhaps dehydrating. Chaga mushrooms cling to the sides of birch trees and have an intense aroma that is almost overly concentrated when dehydrated. Mushrooms are a little like flowers, where one blanket technique won't work for each one—you'll have to discover the best techniques by trial and error. The best place to start is to add the mushroom to the end of the boil and allow it to steep in a whirlpool for 15 or 20 minutes before transferring; or, dehydrate the mushrooms and then rehydrate before adding to the fermenter.

Bark

We spent most of 2015 experimenting with trees and tree barks. We started with hickory, since Ryan had read about using it in a smoky, incense-like syrup. We tried the technique in a Scottish 80 Shilling Ale and were blown away by the results. This led us down a rabbit hole, experimenting with every bark we could get our hands on in the woods around the brewery. For the most part, we enhanced the bark by toasting it before boiling it, and the barks were generally better when boiled for 60 minutes. But some, like wild cherry bark,

were better green off the tree. And bark from Eastern red cedar was better untoasted, as it had a tendency to burn. Shagbark hickory worked best for us, since its bark is shaggy (hence the name) and easy to harvest—and as a bonus, if you pull pieces that are nearly falling off, you won't hurt the tree. Be sure to check a plant guide before using bark to make sure that it's not toxic. We've had interesting results using bark from sycamore, maple, birch, oak, wild cherry, hickory, and Eastern red cedar. We generally toast in an oven at around 350 degrees Fahrenheit for 40 minutes, until the bark smells very aromatic. The timing depends on the thickness of the bark, and how dry it is. But it will still be different for every tree, so keep a close eye on your bark as it bakes.

Sap

In the chapter on sugar maple (page 32) we explore in detail how to extract sap from the tree and brew with it. Many trees—birch and box elder are two others—can be "sugared" in precisely the same way that maple can. This is a process that always happens toward the end of winter as the weather warms and the sap begins to flow abundantly. We have used sap entirely interchangeably with water, using it as one normally would for mashing and sparging with great results.

Heed the advice in the maple chapter for usage of all varieties of sap, and remember that the greatest difference between sap and water isn't the fact that sap has sugar, but that it has a totally unknown mineral content that you won't know precisely on your brew day. Our experience with maple and birch sap has led us to create beers with robust malt profiles that seem to complement the mysterious chemistry of our sap, and we would advise taking a similar tack. We have found lighter beers to taste medicinal, sometimes metallic, and lightly astringent.

Branches and Stems

When we cook with herbs we usually remove the leaves from the stem. We do this for texture more than for flavor—stems can be tough, woody, difficult to chop, and often hard to chew. However, the stems of herbs and the branches of trees offer just as much flavor as the leaves themselves, and in brewing we don't care about texture. This just gives us another tool we can work with.

In our experience, flavor sometimes follows texture with branches and stems: some that are coarser taste more woody (larger juniper branches strike us this way); but sometimes the flavor is just slightly askew of what we're used to and offers something even better. For instance, we've found that the leaves and stems of lavender offer a lighter, almost vanilla and cinnamon-like version of the plant we think we know. Rather than floral and soapy flavors that are easy to get from the flower, we find material even better adapted to beer-making in the leaves and stem.

Every branch and stem will be a little bit different, so experiment—steep some of them to learn what they might give. When harvesting birch sap one morning, we noticed sap leaking from a branch that had been slightly damaged on the side of the tree. We cut that branch and a couple more and added it to the beer to find that it gave a fresh, green bitterness. After fermentation and as the beer was young, we noticed a slight rubbery quality, a little off-putting. However, as the beer conditioned for the next six months, the rubberiness mellowed out and we were left with the flavor we originally tasted in the tree. The flavor of the branches, like so many other ingredients we may use, can evolve over time.

Juniper branches have been used for centuries in Nordic brewing as a way to filter and flavor beer. (Find more details on this technique in the chapter on juniper starting on page 4.) Juniper is particularly well adapted for this use because of

the same way, but adding them to the hot liquor tank or on top of the grains in your mash will help infuse their flavors in a different way than by simply boiling.

Leaves

Let us turn everything you think you know about flavoring on its head: you can boil herbs and still maintain flavor and aroma.

This may seem counterintuitive to hop heads, and this rule is certainly not true of hops. But hops are just one plant that has been studied extensively in beer-making. There are so many plants that haven't been rigorously studied in brewing, and they all function a little bit differently. Dr. Matt McCarroll, the director of the Fermentation Science Institute at Southern Illinois University, explains:

> On a simple level, different plants have various oils that can differ in their boiling point, aqueous solubility, and chemical reactivity. These differences can determine the degree to which compounds are maintained through the brewing process and in the finished beer. The scenario is further complicated by the myriad transformations that can take place either through direct chemical reactions or biotransformation as part of yeast metabolism during fermentation, as is now known to occur with aroma compounds derived from hop additions. Additionally, differing sensory thresholds and the phenomena of flavor and aroma masking obfuscate a simple prediction of the resulting beer.

In other words, we know a lot about how hops are volatilized in the boil and their reactions during fermentation, but we know a lot less about other plants because of their different chemical makeup. But this also makes it an exciting avenue of brewing and one we hope to see research into in the future.

When we brew at Scratch, we don't necessarily

the web-like leaves that shoot off from the main branch, and the fact that it is fantastically aromatic. But juniper does not by any means have a monopoly over this technique! Try using other types of branches from the *Juniperus* genus of trees, or other evergreens like pine and spruce. Try branches from trees like oak, hickory, or maple in your mash. They may not act as filters in quite

know the precise chemistry of all the plants we use, or how their essential oils interact with boiling and fermentation processes. Many times, we discover this by our own perception and by trial and error. Again, lavender is a great example of what we have learned through experimentation: added at the end of the boil, the flowers in particular impart a soapy, floral quality. However, boiling the leaves and stems for 60 minutes gives a beguiling vanilla-cinnamon-cherry character. In fact, herbs added at the end of the boil often seem to us to give a superficial aroma that dies back quickly. In our basil beer, for instance, we add basil in several additions at the beginning, middle, and end of the boil, and often in the mash and hot liquor tank. In our experience, this serves to infuse the flavor and aroma more deeply into the beer.

Many herbs, and especially leaves from trees, also have some bittering potential. This hasn't been studied scientifically as far as we know, but through experimentation in our beer we have found bitterness in leaves from trees like oak and hickory, often in combination with a light tannic quality. Oak and hickory make great substitutions for hop bitterness, as they have a slightly sharper bitterness than, say, dandelion or basil. Just remember that most plants don't have the same anti-microbial properties as hops, so if you bitter with something other than hops, you'll either want to add a few hops for bittering, or supplement later at the flavoring stage to help preserve the beer against infection. You may also consider just letting the beer go sour. We have found that letting the beer sour naturally after adding some plants for bittering actually creates a clean lactobacillic sourness that can be very pleasant. To date, with proper sanitation methods on our fermenters and hoses, all of our beers made without hops sour naturally and taste clean and refreshing. Proper sanitation should at least help guard against some of the bad bacteria that may

infect your beer, and fermenting with a *Saccharomyces* yeast strain to start will get the alcohol content up and sugar content down so that the bad bacteria have a smaller chance of taking over.

Flowers

Flowers are one of the more finicky plant parts you can add to beer. Too many, and your beer might taste like children's cough syrup; too little, and the flowery flavors are lost entirely. Add to that the fact that every flower is slightly different from the next—a little more or less aromatic—and it's hard to come up with a good guideline that will work for every beer.

The best advice on adding flowers to beer has more to do with harvesting than it does with quantity. Flowers are delicate not only because of their aroma, but because there is actually a relatively small window when they're at their peak for harvest. One thing that seems to be universal in our experience is that flowers should be used in beer within only a couple of hours of harvesting. Their aroma begins to change almost immediately after being picked. You've probably noticed that freshly cut flowers will wilt and turn brown and begin to give off that "dead flower" smell quickly if not kept in water. The same is true of any other flower you may pick for beer. Think about this as you're adding it to the wort!

Often the window in which your flower is at its peak may not be more than a couple of weeks. Why are flowers so deceiving? They seem so abundant one day—honeysuckle stretching across the edge of a lawn as far as the eye can see—and gone by your next brew day. Try to keep an eye on flowers as you begin to see them popping up around you. Plan on brewing with them as soon as they look abundant and are fully blooming. This goes for the time of year as much as for the time of day. Some flowers open more widely in the morning; others more

widely around midday. For peak aroma, pick them when they appear most full and open; and pick flowers that are bright and colorful, not brown or wilted. Elderflower is a particularly delicate flower in this sense, giving off a kind of rotten lemon rind aroma when not picked fully white. Also, harvest flowers after the morning dew has evaporated—the blooms should be fairly dry, so they won't get musty.

There is one exception to the fresh flower rule: drying. Dried flowers often keep their aroma (or a slightly altered version of their aroma) for a long time if stored in an airtight container. We particularly like the way that elderflower changes as it dries—it becomes slightly almond-like. We've kept it for years in a mason jar and added it sparingly

to beers. Japanese honeysuckle is another flower that has been used in Asian cultures for a variety of ailments, and can be found dried at health stores or international grocery stores. If you dry the flowers yourself, be sure to give them lots of space so that air can pass around their petals. This will help keep them from getting musty.

As for the precise quantity of flowers to add to beer, this is something you will have to discover as you go along. Flowers are one ingredient where it makes sense to overestimate and dial back the next time. Usually your first estimate won't quite be enough. However, in general we find that a flower that is particularly aromatic on the bush or vine will also be aromatic in beer.

Fruit

After the flowers have passed their lifespan for many plants, it's on to the fruits. In southern Illinois we have wild-growing elderberries, blackberries, raspberries, paw paws, and loads of peaches and apples from surrounding orchards. We have also found people regionally growing less common fruits like gooseberries, aronia berries, and currants. Much has been written about using fruits in beer, usually in a secondary fermentation, and we find this to be a good method. In general it seems that adding fruit at a rate of 2 pounds per gallon is an adequate place to start; you can dial up or down depending on your taste. As an additional technique, we can add fruit to the end of the boil as opposed to the fermenter. There is some loss of flavor this way, but it helps to guard against infection.

Most fruit can be frozen, a big benefit we definitely appreciate for allowing us to brew with certain fruits when they would otherwise be out of season. With some fruits—apples, peaches, and paw paws, in particular—we've also had great success caramelizing the fruit and adding it to the fermenter. This adds a whole other layer of complexity and also guards against infection.

There isn't any citrus that grows near us, but lemons have been used for centuries in beer to add extra acidity. Citrus in general—not just lemons, but also oranges, grapefruit, kumquats, tangerines—is a great complement to other flavors (it's especially good with ginger) and to peppery or fruity yeast strains. The rind has more aromatic qualities than the flesh, so grating the rind and adding it to the beer will give that citrus aroma without the extra acidity of using the pulp. We usually grate the rind and juice the pulp and add them both to the last 5 minutes of the boil.

Seeds

We use a handful of seeds year-round in our beer, and there are hundreds of others that have potential that we have yet to try. Pumpkin seeds are one of our favorites. Toasted until golden and added to the fermenter, they give an incredible toasty and nutty character that enhances bready malts. We prefer using these over the meat of the pumpkin, and you can use any kind of squash seed the same way.

Lotus seeds are much less common, but also give a nice nutty aroma when toasted. Wild carrot seeds have been infused in beer for centuries to add apricot flavor. In general, we think toasting seeds helps to bring out toasty aroma (like sesame or sunflower seeds), but each seed is different and tastes a lot like the plant from which it springs. Some are spicier (caraway or coriander), some more peppery (peppercorn or chile seeds). Be careful, because some (like apple seeds) are toxic. Others, like chile seeds, carry all of the heat of the plant—you can either make your beer hotter by using them in place of the chile, or make the chile tamer by removing the seeds entirely.

Nuts

Nuts that grow abundantly in our area include some more familiar varieties like walnut and pecan, and some less common in culinary use, like acorns and hickory nuts. In general, nuts have a substantial amount of oil, which can negatively affect mouthfeel and head retention when used in beer. Our friends at Piney River Brewing in Bucyrus, Missouri, use walnuts in their fantastic Black

Walnut Wheat. (Hammons, the biggest black walnut producer in the world, is just around the corner from them, so they have a steady supply.) They add the nuts to the mash, which brewmaster Brian Dunham says allows him to draw out a lovely hint of walnut while maintaining a substantial white head. This seems a good base process for any oily nut.

Other nuts, like acorns and hickory nuts, don't suffer from an overabundance of oil, but they do present other challenges. Acorns, for example, are exceedingly astringent and must be leached first to release their bitter tannins. We have used acorns (after lengthy processing) as a flour, but the best way of all to incorporate acorns may be in an unexpected form: fermented. Fermented acorns have an unbelievable aroma of oak, leather, madeira, prunes, and bourbon. We were lucky to stumble upon their flavor inside a mason jar we kept closed for over a year.

Hickory nuts are also abundant on our property. They fall from the tree green and are easily hulled at that point because the husks break apart a bit like an orange. After spending some time on the ground, hickory nuts will dry up, turn brown, and crack open naturally—although they lose a little bit of their bitterness and nutty character. We use them in both their green and brown stages. Hickory nuts are interesting: they are bitter, but not as bitter as walnuts; nutty, but not as nutty as peanuts; and they have very little oil content. Overall, they are relatively delicate, but make a fantastic addition to beer, smoothing out golden ales, maibocks, or lagers. We use them a lot in our hickory beers as a bittering component, and for flavor and aroma. Acorns and hickory nuts are good examples of unexpected nuts that have their own unique flavor profile, very different from peanuts, walnuts, or pecans, and emblematic of numerous trees with similar potential.

Creating Gruits

In ancient and pre-medieval times, dozens, if not hundreds, of different plants were used in beer-making. The plants people brewed with were distinctive markers of the region where beer was produced: heather, bog myrtle, yarrow, wormwood, spruce. A gruit (or similar derivation of the name) is the historical term for a beer brewed without hops, with particular reference to medieval Germany. The Archbishop of Cologne had a monopoly over gruit production (and the resulting taxes) and thus had an interest in seeing this style of beer proliferate, particularly in opposition to the new hopped beers that were beginning to be produced at the time, outside of ecclesiastical regulation. Gruits and hopped beers were thus originally part of a dynamic power struggle between German states and the church. We use the term at our brewery today to refer simply to a beer brewed without hops, usually using a combination of several different plants.

Brewing without hops has been an exciting avenue of brewing for us. It has brought some of the most intriguing flavors, and taught us the most about the bittering, flavoring, and aroma potential of plants. We approach brewing gruits in two different ways. First are beers that are structured in many ways like the beer we know today, with perceivable bittering, flavoring, and aroma components. For these beers we often choose a plant (or several plants) that have significant bittering potential and use them at the beginning of the boil. Often we use roots for this, or something slightly tannic, or a bitter green. Next, we'll find something that will complement the malt or yeast character as a flavoring or aroma component. More often than not we choose plants that are in season, although sometimes we'll use a plant that's been dried or frozen. For us, gruits are about the bounty of the season—combining what's growing around us in interesting ways. We tend to do more of these in the spring and summer than in the fall and winter. Our Spring Tonic—a beer brewed without hops (see page 48)—is a celebration of the new green popping up around the brewery, usually around late March or early April.

The second approach we take to brewing gruits is brewing something we intend to go sour. This may be a beer into which we pitch a *Lactobacillus*

culture directly, or a beer we brew with a *Saccharomyces* yeast, which will eventually go sour. These beers aren't necessarily brewed with a specific bittering ingredient in mind, but with the goal of blending plant character with the lemony tartness of lactic acid. There have been some surprising revelations in this regard. Our Single Tree: Hickory was a beer that turned sour over time without the addition of hops, and turned into one of our absolute favorite beers. The marshmallow and incense quality of the toasted hickory bark was a surprising complement to the sweet-tart lacto culture. We rarely re-brew a beer twice in the same year but ended up re-brewing that one three times, both allowing it to go sour after pitching a *Saccharomyces* yeast, and by pitching a mixed culture with *Lactobacillus* and letting it go to town.

Preserving

Having looked at all the parts of the plant from the ground up, the only thing that's left to mention is how to extend the lives of these ingredients for our purposes year-round. We do a lot of preserving at the brewery, often using herbs and plants the way one would use spice additions for cooking. When you've built up a library of dried plants, you have a trove of options on your brew day: You can enhance the nutty flavor of a malt or hickory hull with dried elderflowers, or complement fresh raspberries with sundried cherry tomatoes.

To dehydrate and preserve herbs and other leafy parts of the plant, we use one of three methods. We set the plant over a screen and allow air to pass through (often aided with a fan, the way you might do for hops); we tie together the bottoms of plants we've pulled out of the ground, and hang them over a wire that runs along the length of our tasting room; or we dry the plants in a dehydrator and pack them into a mason jar. As long as all of the moisture is out of the plant, it will keep in a mason jar without molding indefinitely. We usually use plants that have been hanging in the tasting room within about a year, although even after two or three years, they retain a surprising amount of flavor if they're stored out of direct sunlight.

For other parts of the plants where it's important to retain moisture, such as fruits or some roots (as with ginger and turmeric), we put the plant in the freezer in a sealed bag. It will get a little freezer burn over time, so it's best to get as much oxygen out of the bag as possible, but it will still stay good for a year or more.

You can also preserve some plant flavor and aroma by making an alcoholic tincture. You'll want to infuse your flavors into a neutral grain spirit. A great way of thinking about this process is as if you were making a liqueur or bitters. Stuff a mason jar with a combination of herbs, fruits, even walnuts (nocino is one of our favorite liqueurs, made with green walnuts, and is an excellent addition to beer). Let the combination steep for a couple of weeks until you like the flavor, then filter out the plants. The alcohol will preserve the flavor for years.

Now that you have an overview of general techniques, delve into the next chapters as new plants come into their growing season. We give more detailed information about harvesting specific plants and details about using each part of the plant in brewing in the chapters to follow. Plants are organized by the general season in which they ripen in the middle part of the Midwest, where we're located, although many plants can be used throughout all the seasons—roots during one time of year, leaves during another, flowers and fruits

during yet another. We have guides at the beginning of each season to help you keep track of what to gather when. Your experience with seasons may vary in different parts of the country, with some plants flowering earlier or later than in our region. However, the advice for using each plant will be the same.

Finally, a note on the recipes. All recipes assume a brewhouse efficiency of around 70 percent, although your equipment will probably vary in some of the details. We generally set up our recipes for brewing in old stainless steel kegs, which many homebrewers utilize. On the whole, most details should be roughly similar. Unless otherwise stated, recipes are for a single-infusion mash and all temperatures are in degrees Fahrenheit. Do not be bound by bittering hop suggestions; you can use any one of a number of different hops to bitter. Flavor and aroma hops are more important but you should use all of ours as suggestions, and try different flavor combinations with the plants in each chapter. Sometimes the most surprising combinations work best. We include a total International Bittering Unit (IBU) count so that you can work with the hops you have to reach similar bittering potential—we do not include them as a strict guideline. We often add salts to our water to boost the calcium and balance its natural alkalinity, but we realize that everybody's water chemistry is a little bit different, so we leave those decisions up to you. To finish the boil, we always add a whirlfloc tablet or Irish moss at flameout to help with clarity.

Happy experimenting!

THE
HOMEBREWER'S
ALMANAC

WINTER

Winter may appear to be a hard season for gathering, but the air is crisp and ticks and mosquitoes are dormant. The majority of leaves are off the trees here in southern Illinois, and it's the only time we can see deep into the woods. Walks in the winter can be especially helpful as scouting trips to identify places to return to in another season to gather plants. You can also gather and use green tips of pine, spruce, or juniper trees. Winter is also a time to make use of the abundance of what you have gathered and preserved throughout the year.

WHAT TO LOOK FOR:

Tree Barks: Oak, Hickory, Pecan, Maple, Birch, Cedar, Sycamore, Wild Cherry

Dead Leaves: Maple, Hickory, Oak, Pine Needles

Stalks and Brambles: Grass, Hay, Dried Herbs, Shiso, Grapevine, Rose, Blackberry, Raspberry

Roots: Dock, Chicory, Rose, Blackberry

Dried Wild Berries: Black Raspberry, Hackberry, Spicebush, Rose Hips, Wild Grape

Nuts: Acorns, Hickory, Pecan, Walnut, Chestnut, Pine Nuts

Seeds: Sumac, Shiso

Mushrooms: Oyster

Conifers: Branch Tips, Pine Cones

Stored Foods: Apple, Squash, Sweet Potato, Beet, Turnip, Dried Herbs

Farm and Market: Cabbage, Parsnip, Burdock, Winter Squash, Winter Radish, Salsify

JUNIPER

Evergreen Southern Illinois. The terms couldn't be more opposed. The Pacific Northwest, Norway—these are places bathed in pines year round. The southern Illinois woods, on the contrary, become slate gray in the winter: barren, icy, only dusted with snow. The densest parts of the Shawnee or the Ozarks, where in summer anything more than 12 inches in front of you becomes opaque green, become denuded woody caverns echoing with woodpecker calls and spotted with deer prints by January.

Along certain stretches of backcountry road and abandoned pastureland, however, one may find a cedar—perhaps a few, growing along a fence row—gleaming in the landscape. Not to be confused with Northern white cedar (a toxic member belonging to the cypress family) Eastern red cedar, the "cedar" we find most commonly here, is in fact a juniper. *Juniperus virginiana* is the eastern variety of juniper more often used to make fenceposts, incense, and pencils. It is native, common, and often invasive, but it is a unique sight for us in January when all other trees have receded to their spindly winter frames. The forest hibernates, yet cedar tips retain their emerald pigment and crisp, orange peel aroma. They are one of the few living organisms that promise of life and the spring to come.

Norwegian and Finnish brewing traditions are deeply indebted to the evergreen.

Both make abundant use of juniper—particularly its branches and leaves—as a way of filtering and (they believed) preserving their beer. Juniper was infused into the water and layered beneath the grains of beers brewed in farmhouses. The result is the essence of the forest: a piney green, gin-like flavor that showcases what is for Nordic countries the most felicitous tool and ingredient available. We use this technique often in our beer, and also use the bark and berries in ways that can add complexity. The tips and techniques below translate well for anyone who has other species of juniper in their midst.

HARVESTING

Tips and Branches

The beauty of juniper—and any other evergreen—is that its green spindly tips are available to the brewer year-round. That said, we have noticed slight variations in flavor at different times of the year, with some of the freshest orange scent coming in the spring. Depending on your climate and location, you may notice variations, too. We find it best to pick the greenest tips for the fullest aroma, no matter when they're harvested. The tips can add a surprising sweetness to the finish of the beer.

The tips are the parts that come off a thicker main branch. Cut them where they branch off, and by all means keep the berries if there are some growing. Cutting bigger branches can give an astringent woody character that is less welcome.

Bark

Cedar wood has a very pronounced flavor and aroma, one that often calls to mind its use in furniture to combat mustiness. We've had a customer who can't drink the beers we make with cedar because it reminds him of his brother's hamster cage. You may not associate cedar with hamsters or your grandmother's sweater drawer, but even if you enjoy the aroma it's likely best in small doses.

To avoid overkill, we use the bark that's fallen off a tree or collected from dead trees. The bark has a more subtle woodiness and a slight menthol-like flavor combined with a light tannic bitterness, much more subtle than the wood. Also, harvesting fallen bark or bark from dead trees keeps us from killing a live tree. While we often toast bark to enhance its flavor, we add this one raw so as not to burn it. It requires no other preparation before use.

Berries

About the only part of the tree that's not available year-round are the berries. Depending on your tree, you may be overwhelmed with berries, or it may take hours to collect enough for a batch. Collecting them can be extremely tedious. They are in the best condition for brewing when they are white on the outside and plump. Crushing them very lightly, just a pulse in the food processor, is the best way to open up their flavor. It's best to use the berries fresh; they don't preserve well when stored in jars but can be frozen.

BREWING

Tips and Branches

There are an impressive variety of ways to use juniper tips and branches throughout the brewing process. The first, outlined in the sidebar, is to use them to help filter your mash. You would be amazed at how much flavor and aroma comes through by this simple technique before the boil has even begun.

We prefer to infuse the juniper at a number of points during the process. We heat our mash water with a handful of branches, add a handful of branches to the mash, add a handful of "first wort" branches as we run the mash into the kettle, and then add branches at 60 minutes, 30, and flameout. The result is a beer with a deeply infused juniper character with aromas of pine, orange peel, and gin.

Bark

When used in small quantities juniper bark can add complexity as a bittering agent and harmonize with the branches and berries. It is preferable in a darker beer—amber to black—where it will blend with more highly kilned malts. About an ounce per 5-gallon batch will add subtle complexity. Add it in a mesh bag 60 minutes before the end of the boil.

Berries

Out of the whole tree the berries add the most gin-like punch. Adding them straight from the tree, lightly crushed, toward the end of the boil—10 minutes or less—is the best way to showcase their powerful aromatics. They are a fantastic substitute for piney American hop varieties and in general make an excellent complement to other hops. We make very few IPAs but one we make every year is a Cedar IPA utilizing the berries. We've tried a variety of hops in concert, often some of the more citrusy ones, to harmonize but not mimic the cedar character: Citra, Chinook, and Hallertau, to name a few.

The berries can also be roasted to varying degrees to add another level of complexity. For a 5-gallon batch, heat an oven to 350 degrees Fahrenheit and toast a half ounce of the berries for 15 minutes to give a slightly chocolatey flavor, or 30 minutes for something more sharp and coffee-like. Crush them lightly and add to the end of the boil, or to the fermenter. Adding to the fermenter will allow you to keg or bottle the beer at just the point you prefer the mix of flavors and aromas. They should sink to the bottom of your vessel so you can rack off the top.

The recipes included here are for two of our favorite juniper beers. The Cedar IPA makes use of the berries exclusively, while the Sahti utilizes our method for infusing juniper character throughout the brewing process. Our Sahti is not a traditional Finnish sahti, but is inspired by those flavors and traditions, as well as the bready, spicy rye we get from Riverbend Malt House in North Carolina. Use it as a jumping off point for your own juniper-infused beers.

FILTERING THE MASH THROUGH JUNIPER

Using juniper branches as a filter for the mash is a generations-old technique for Norwegian homebrewers and Finnish sahti makers. Odd Nordland's comprehensive 1969 work about beer and brewing traditions in Norway showed that the majority of Norwegian brewers (most of whom brewed at home on family plots and farms) used juniper, straw, or even hair to filter their mash. Finnish sahti makers in contrast filter the mash through a *kuurna*, a hollowed out log lined with juniper branches under the grain.

Homebrewers can go as deeply into the traditional process as they want. Here are two simple suggestions about how to approximate these techniques in home brewing:

1. Infuse mash water and/or sparge water with juniper, and add branches to the mash

Water in the hot liquor tank is also often infused with juniper in Nordic traditions, and the flavor will come through at the end of the boil. This and a layer of branches at the top of the mash tun will give lots of character without the somewhat more difficult process of layering under the mash. A couple of branches in the mash water, mash, and sparge water will do the trick. If you will not be adding cedar tips or berries later to the boil, consider adding four or five more branches to enhance the flavor.

This method also works for extract brewers. Put a couple branches in the kettle while heating the water, and leave them there if steeping specialty grains. Remove the branches before boiling, but feel free to add fresh branches during the boil.

2. Layer branches above the false bottom in your mash tun

This is an easy step for all-grain brewers: the false bottom can be used as a fail-safe for the grain while providing a perfect basket to hold the juniper beneath the mash. Put branches criss-crossing above the false bottom, followed by the grain. Mash in with your water over the grains. Note that to do this, you must add water to the grains rather than the grains to the water in the mash tun in order to keep the juniper stable under the grain bed. Otherwise the juniper will float to the top. Also consider using straw in combination with the juniper, or as an alternative filter. Better still, use hay. Hay has the added benefit of a fantastic cherry and tobacco aroma that can add an extra dimension to your beer.

You can get as complex as you like from here. Some sahti makers do a decoction (or several) to raise the temperature of their mash from around 130 to 149 degrees Fahrenheit, before straining everything through the *kuurna*.

CEDAR IPA

Batch Size: 5 gallons
OG: 1.068
FG: 1.010
ABV: 7.7%
Bitterness: 50 IBU

GRAINS

11 pounds Maris Otter
1 pound Munich
11 ounces crystal 40°Lovibond

MASH

Mash in with 5 gallons water to hit 150 degrees Fahrenheit
Sparge with 6 gallons water at 168 degrees Fahrenheit

HOPS

¾ ounce Nugget at 60 minutes
½ ounce Chinook at 15 minutes
½ ounce Chinook at 10 minutes
½ ounce Chinook at 5 minutes
1½ ounces Chinook dry hop

ADDITIONAL INGREDIENTS

3 ounces crushed juniper berries at flameout

LENGTH OF BOIL

60 minutes

YEAST

American Ale

FERMENTATION

Pitch at 68 degrees Fahrenheit. Hold for one week and allow to rise above 70 degrees.

Add 1½ ounces of Chinook to the fermenter for three days after primary fermentation is complete. Add more juniper berries after primary fermentation to boost aroma if desired.

SAHTI

Batch Size: 5 gallons
OG: 1.063
FG: 1.012
ABV: 6.7%
Bitterness: 22 IBU

GRAINS
6 pounds 5 ounces Vienna
2 pounds 10 ounces Munich
1 pound rye
1 pound Pilsner
10 ounces chocolate malt
4 ounces Special B

MASH
Mash in with 4½ gallons water to hit
   150 degrees Fahrenheit
Sparge with 6 gallons water at
   168 degrees Fahrenheit

HOPS
½ ounce Nugget at 60 minutes
½ ounce Willamette at 20 minutes

ADDITIONAL INGREDIENTS
1 (10–12-inch-long) juniper branch in
   hot liquor tank
1 juniper branch in mash
1 juniper branch at 60 minutes
1 juniper branch at 30 minutes
6 juniper branches at flameout

LENGTH OF BOIL
60 minutes with 15-minute whirlpool at
   end of boil

YEAST
British Ale

FERMENTATION
Pitch at 68 degrees Fahrenheit. Hold for one week and allow to rise above 70 degrees until fermentation is complete.

GRAPEVINE

If you know even a small amount about wine, you know that there are a variety of different grapes that create different flavors and aromas when crushed and fermented. These grapes flourish in all kinds of different growing conditions across the world. Well, the vast majority of those grapes are within the *Vitis vinifera* species, a species of grape that's native to Europe. The United States has a number of other native species of *Vitis* that grow wild—some well adapted to traditional wine-making, some not. But the plant as a whole is very interesting for beer.

We won't belabor the many ways grapes have been used in wine-making, but we will point out a few of the more unusual ways the plant has been consumed. The leaves and bark have been used by Native Americans for medicinal teas, and even used topically for skin-related conditions. Today it's fairly easy to find grappa, a spirit from Italy that is a distillate of the pomace (grape skins, seeds, and stems) from wine-making. There are also many historical recipes for raisin wine, as well as for a drink called Persencia, which was a fermented concoction of raisins and milk.

In this chapter we explore the whole grapevine, from the grapes to the leaves to the vine. It is a plant that we find throughout our woods that seems to grow well in the eastern half of the United States, although Canyon grape (*Vitis arizonica*), California grape (*Vitis californica*), and Valley grape

(*Vitis girdiana*) are species that grow wild in the American southwest and parts of Mexico. Cultivated grapes of the *Vitis vinifera* species of course also grow well along the west coast of the United States, all over California, Oregon, and Washington. Any of these techniques can be applied to *Vitis vinifera,* as well as any wild grape that grows near you.

HARVESTING

Vine

A grapevine growing wild looks a lot like the grapevine you may have seen dozens of times in a vineyard. The only difference is that it's not trained on a wire—it may be growing around the branches of a tree!—making it perhaps a surprising and unusual plant to find in the woods. You may not know exactly what species of *Vitis* plant you have found, but fortunately there aren't very many plants that look like grapes growing in the wild. Some non-grapevine vines, like poison oak—which also grows on trees and can be quite thick as it ages—are hairy and stick to the side of the tree, unlike grapevines, which hang rather than cling. (Poison oak also lacks clustered fruit.)

Two clustered fruits that may resemble grapes are sumac and pokeberry, but neither of these grow on a vine. Edible sumac, which you can read about on page 90, is always red, so you cannot make a toxic mistake if you choose the red variety because you mistook it for grapes (the berries are small and dense and do not otherwise resemble a grape at all). Pokeberries, on the other hand, look similar to a deep purple grape. But they grow on a magenta stalk, and their berries are not as densely clustered as grapes. Their leaves are also ovate and do not resemble grape leaves, which look quite similar to a hop leaf. Pokeberries are not edible. In Oregon there is a native plant, commonly called Oregon grape, which is edible and even used for wine, although it is not a true grape. It is a shrub as opposed to a vine, with a leaf that is spiny and resembles holly.

We harvest grapevines throughout the year, though we often gather them in the winter since they are one of the plants we can still identify. Sometimes it's even easier to find grapevines in winter, without all the other foliage in the woods. Grapevines are also easy to find when they are fruiting, since the grape clusters are their calling card and hard to mistake for anything else. We take mental notes of where we see grapevines in the early fall, then come back later in the winter to harvest the vine. Just like you see in vineyards, the older the vine, the thicker it will be; some can be decades old and five or six inches thick. The best way to harvest a grapevine is to use prunings throughout the year. You can do this yourself on a vine in the woods. Or if there are vineyards near you, ask for prunings of the plant during the growing season. It's best to use a vine that hasn't been sprayed with pesticides and herbicides.

Leaves

We've used grape leaves in both green and brown stages, as with many tree leaves in this book. Grape leaves are a wonderful bittering ingredient, and contain a classic tannin flavor you might only expect from the fruit. Harvest in the summer when they are full and green, or in the late fall when the fruit is gone and the plant is going dormant for the winter.

Grapes

Grapes can be harvested and used like any other fruit. One recent trend is to blend the fruit, juice, or the must into the brewing process to create a beer that is as wine-like as it is beer-like. To do so, the grapes should be harvested when they're at their peak for sugar and acidity—essentially when the fruit is at its best for wine making. Having wine-makers nearby will help with this process, and hopefully they will be willing to part with some of their harvest in exchange for a bottle or two of beer.

When harvesting grapes from the wild, it will be up to your taste buds to decide when it's best to harvest. We've found that wild grapes tend to mature a little later than their cultivated cousins. If there is a grapevine near you, taste the fruit beginning in the early fall and pick the grapes when the flavor is to your liking. A lot of wild grapes are astringent and even a little musty and may not be ideal for brewing. Taste test before adding to beer.

However, there are benefits to letting the grapes sit on the vine past their peak ripeness. They can be harvested in the middle of autumn, which allows cold temperatures to concentrate the sugars—wine-makers will use these grapes to make ice wine. (As an alternative, harvest when the grapes are at their peak and then let them dry over the course of a couple of weeks, similar to the method for making Amarone.) Leaving them alone even longer, into the late fall, creates something like a sweet raisin. We've sometimes found these little raisin-like grapes among the dead leaves on the forest floor in the middle of the winter, perfectly fit for brewing—though past their prime for wine-making.

BREWING

Vine

We absolutely love using grapevine in beer. It was one of the plants we tried while on our bark-brewing kick, and we were amazed at the results. In beer, the vine imparts a number of the same qualities it can add to wine; tannins, in particular, as well as other phenolic compounds. These are flavors you might be familiar with in grappa.

But we also toast the vine the way we toast hickory bark, and this results in a host of other flavors as well, most prominently a smoky vanillin character. Over time, the resulting brew even tastes a little bit like grapes. We have enjoyed this in beers as diverse as a sour blonde beer and a malty wee heavy. To toast the vine, harvest about a 3-foot section and chop it into 1-inch cubes.

(Use a similar amount of grapevine prunings as an alternative.) Toast in an oven at 350 degrees Fahrenheit for about an hour or until the vine becomes incense-like and aromatic. Add to the fermenter after primary fermentation once the vine has cooled slightly, and sample after about a week. Rack when the flavor is to your liking.

Leaves

Bitter with grape leaves the same way that we suggest for hickory (page 138) or oak (page 150). Boil about half a pound for 60 minutes for a 5-gallon batch. You can often find grape leaves in international grocery stores, as they are often used for wrapping foods in Mediterranean cuisine. However, these leaves are usually preserved in a solution, and therefore not ideal to use as a bittering ingredient for beer.

Grapes

Grapes can be used just like any other fruit. When fresh from the vine they can be mashed and the juice, skins, and seeds can all be added to the beer, depending on the effect you're trying to achieve. For the most part, this addition is probably best in the fermenter, given the seeming delicacy of the aromas and the extraction of tannins you may not want to enhance by boiling. Remember that the skins and seeds are where most of the tannins reside, so they will not only color your beer but will also add extra bitterness. The sugar will also cause the beer to re-ferment, so you may want to either rack off the skins into another fermenter if you don't want too much tannin character in your beer. Or just let it ride, perhaps adding fewer hops in the bittering stage.

Wild grapes that you might have harvested in a raisin-like state can be added to the fermenter or to the end of the boil. Any grape you add to the fermenter will likely inoculate the beer with a wild yeast strain, so be prepared for the fermentation character to change. To attempt to avoid this secondary inoculation, try bringing the grapes up to 180 degrees Fahrenheit for about 15 minutes in a little bit of water to keep them from burning. Then allow them to cool slightly and add them to the fermenter.

WILD GRAPEVINE WEE HEAVY

Batch Size: 5 gallons
OG: 1.075
FG: 1.016
ABV: 7.8%
Bitterness: 20 IBU

GRAINS
11 pounds 10 ounces Maris Otter
1 pounds 10 ounces Munich
6 ounces crystal 80°L
6 ounces roasted barley

MASH
Mash in with 5½ gallons water to hit
    150 degrees Fahrenheit
Sparge with 5½ gallons water at
    168 degrees Fahrenheit

HOPS
½ ounce Nugget at 60 minutes

ADDITIONAL INGREDIENTS
One 3-foot-long section of grapevine,
    chopped into 1-inch cubes and
    toasted, added to the fermenter

LENGTH OF BOIL
60 minutes with 15-minute whirlpool at
    end of boil

YEAST
British Ale

FERMENTATION
*Pitch at 68 degrees Fahrenheit. Hold
for one week and allow to rise above
70 degrees until fermentation is complete.*

*Add the 1-inch cubes of toasted grape-
vine and condition for six months before
drinking.*

WILD ROSE

In truth the wild rose could refer to any one of hundreds of different wild *Rosa* species. The *Rosa virginiana* is the most common wild rose in the United States, but the *Rosa arkansana*, often called the prairie rose, is also well represented, and it grows as far north as Alberta, Canada (where wild roses are abundant). We have a wild swamp rose that grows in our cypress swamps. Your region will have its own local mix of species, and even more cultivated varieties that can be used in similar ways.

Just about every part of the rose has been used for centuries, and it is another plant that offers a variety of different flavor profiles for beer. Wild rose root has long been used as a tea, and it's no wonder. Try steeping it for 10 or 15 minutes in hot water and taste it. It has incredible tannic flavor and is deeply reminiscent of black tea. The flower, of course, has an unmistakable floral aroma. Certain varieties of wild rose are more aromatic than others, but all can be used for their distinctive scent. Finally, rose hips—the sometimes-ignored fruit of the rose plant—give a wonderfully tart, citrusy flavor. Wild rose varieties have smaller hips, but you can cultivate varieties like the *Rosa rugosa*, which bear particularly large fruit, for your brewing purposes. Rose hips are rich in vitamin C, and are a good source for it in locations like ours, where citrus fruits are few and far between.

Wild rose is also a great plant for year-round brewing. The flower is available in the height of the summer; the hips come on in the fall and reach their peak after the first frost; the root is still identifiable in the winter, and makes for an interesting addition during the colder months. The hips also preserve well, making them a good fruit to have on hand any time of the year for beer.

HARVESTING

Root

We usually harvest wild rose root in the winter, as it's one of a handful that we can still identify above ground thanks to its thorny bramble. Be careful of the thorns and use a long spade or shovel to dig deep into the ground to harvest the roots. Rinse off the dirt before brewing. You can brew with the bramble, too. It gives a character similar to the root, although it's a little greener and has less black tea flavor.

Flowers

Flowers are harvested midsummer when wide open at midday. Use them immediately after harvesting.

Hips

Hips grow beneath each flower and can be harvested around early fall, assuming you haven't already harvested all the flowers!

(You can, however, harvest the petals of the flower after the flower has been pollinated and still get a rose hip later in the season, as long as you don't damage the pistil.) You can also dry rose hips to use later in the year. Rose hips have little seeds and hairs on the inside that can irritate if consumed. If you plan on adding the hips to your brew in a bag that will catch the seeds and hairs, you can dry them whole. If you plan on adding them to the fermenter, cut the hips in half and scrape out the seeds and hairs to keep them from floating in your finished product, then dry halved.

BREWING

Root

We boil the root for 60 minutes to extract as much of the tannins as possible. The root adds a lovely bitterness we have enjoyed in amber or rose-colored bières de garde and bières de mars. It benefits from a grain bill that's not heavy on specialty malts but has a little bit of backbone to stand up to the tannins. Use 1½ ounces of the root in a 5-gallon batch.

Flowers

Wild rose is slightly less aromatic than many varieties of cultivated roses, so it's best to use it as soon as it's harvested and best to put it right into the fermenter. The roses should float (a bit like a whole hop flower) so you can rack the beer from underneath. Try using 2 ounces of rose petals as a starting place, and dial up or down depending on your preference.

Hips

Rose hips are tart and are commonly steeped in water for tea. You can use this method for a flameout addition, or steep later in the fermenter. Like so many tart fruits, rose hips are wonderful for dry saison-style beers, or to give dimension to a berlinerweiss or other beer fermented with a light *Lactobacillus* addition. If the beer is already quite sour, the tartness from the rose hips may get lost, so a drier beer like a saison or witbier may actually work a little better. Steep 3 pounds of fresh rose hips or 1 pound of dried rose hips in a 5-gallon batch. Slice in half and add to the boil or the fermenter. It's best to scrape out the inside, so that as few seeds and hairs as possible make it into your final beer. Make sure to use a fine mesh bag in the boil kettle if you don't remove the seeds and hairs.

ROSE ROOT BIÈRE DE MARS

Batch Size: 5 gallons

OG: 1.063

FG: 1.014

ABV: 6.5%

Bitterness: 23 IBU

GRAINS

7 pounds 5 ounces Vienna
2 pounds 10 ounces Pilsner
1 pound 10 ounces Munich
11 ounces Special B
1 ounce black malt

MASH

Mash in with 5 gallons water to hit
150 degrees Fahrenheit
Sparge with 7 gallons water at
168 degrees Fahrenheit

HOPS

½ ounce Nugget at 60 minutes
½ ounce Willamette at 5 minutes

ADDITIONAL INGREDIENTS

1½ ounces rose root at 60 minutes
2 (12-inch-long) spicebush twigs the
thickness of a pencil at 60 minutes
(you can substitute with 1 tablespoon
of allspice, or 1 tablespoon of peppercorns, or a combination of the two)

LENGTH OF BOIL

90 minutes with 15-minute whirlpool at
flameout

YEAST

German Alt

FERMENTATION

*Pitch at 57 degrees Fahrenheit. Hold
for two weeks and allow to rise until
fermentation is complete.*

*Condition for three months before
drinking.*

SWEET POTATO

Sweet potatoes are a staple of many cultures in temperate or tropical climates. In the United States, we tend to think of them as a southern crop. It's true that most sweet potato production is in the south and in California, the two regions with the best temperatures for their growth. But sweet potatoes have been cultivated across the Americas for millennia—and for good reason. They are loaded with vitamins and minerals, and best of all, contain that beta-carotene flavor that tastes so good when roasted with the natural sugars in the potato.

Although often mistaken for one another, sweet potatoes and yams are two different tubers from two different families. However, for the purposes of brewing, they can be used in similar ways. They can be mashed to extract sugars, or roasted and added to the fermenter for flavor. Although very different plants, they produce similar flavor profiles.

Sweet potatoes keep extraordinarily well in a cupboard or cellar, and make a great year-round brewing ingredient. We like using them in the winter with lager yeasts that ferment clean. We also try to use the sweet potato—not usually known for its subtlety—in a more delicate way in the mash, or a little bit in the fermenter.

HARVESTING

Sweet potatoes are generally harvested in the fall after a summer planting. After curing in a warm place for a little over a week, they can be stored for months. If buying from a farmer or at a store, they are usually already in this cured state.

We were given pre-roasted sweet potatoes that had been frozen and found that the flavor suffered compared to sweet potatoes roasted the same day that they were added to the beer—also, the sugar content seemed lower than it should have been. We don't recommend freezing sweet potatoes or using frozen sweet potatoes as an alternative to fresh.

BREWING

Sweet potatoes don't add very much perceptible flavor to a beer when mashed, but they do add some sugar content and a lot of color. The best way to do this is to dice the sweet potatoes and roast them until they start to caramelize. When they start to caramelize, take them out of the oven and mash them with a potato masher until relatively pulpy, with some chunks. Add them to the top of grains when you're mashing in; this way they don't cause the mash to stick. This method has worked well for us without requiring the addition of rice hulls. Sparge like normal. Use about 5 pounds for a 5-gallon batch of beer.

Follow the same initial process to caramelize the sweet potatoes for the fermenter. Dicing the sweet potatoes is a little tedious, but this gives them more surface area, allowing more of the potato to caramelize. Skinning the sweet potatoes before dicing will also help increase the surface area and results in a less earthy, bitter flavor. Once the potatoes are golden brown, pull them from the oven and allow to cool briefly (covered, if possible), and then add them to the fermenter. You won't need a full 5 pounds to notice the flavor. Start with 3 pounds and dial up or down depending on your taste.

The recipe below is for a faux Vienna lager. We like using American Ale yeast fermented at a lower temperature to make a clean, near-hybrid ale when we can't brew a true lager. After a week of steady fermentation in the low sixties (Fahrenheit), we allow the beer to rise naturally in temperature to finish fermenting in the low seventies. Once the beer is finished and there is no perceptible diacetyl, we drop the temperature and keg (or bottle) the beer. This beer won't taste much like sweet potatoes, since they are added to the mash, but it will have a brilliant orange color and just a hint of beta-carotene. To increase the sweet potato character, add a little more roasted potatoes to the fermenter.

SWEET POTATO VIENNA

Batch Size: 5 gallons
OG: 1.046
FG: 1.010
ABV: 4.6%
Bitterness: 23 IBU

GRAINS
4 pounds 8 ounces Vienna
2 pounds 4 ounces Munich
2 pounds Pilsner

MASH
Mash in with 3¾ gallons water to hit
   150 degrees Fahrenheit
Sparge with 6½ gallons water at
   168 degrees Fahrenheit

HOPS
½ ounce Chinook at 60 minutes
1 ounce Hallertauer at 5 minutes

ADDITIONAL INGREDIENTS
5 pounds coarsely mashed, roasted
   sweet potatoes added to mash tun
   with grains

LENGTH OF BOIL
90 minutes with 15-minute whirlpool at
   flameout

YEAST
American Ale

FERMENTATION
*Pitch at 62 degrees Fahrenheit. Hold for
one week, then allow the temperature to
rise naturally into the 70s until fermentation is complete.*

*To increase sweet potato character,
add another 3 pounds of roasted sweet
potatoes to fermenter after primary
fermentation.*

SAGE

Sage was an important brewing herb in the Middle Ages, used to produce beer that was thought to have healing qualities. Garden sage, or *Salvia officinalis*, is the common sage we grow at home. It hails from both sides of the Mediterranean, being native to Spain, France, and the western Balkans, although *Salvia* more generally is found all around the world.

There are 900 different species of *Salvia*, each with its own unique aroma. Some are more obviously suited for brewing than others because of their chemical makeup. A few varieties of garden sage, for instance, like Purpurascens and Tricolor, have alpha-humulene and beta-pinene essential oils that make them very similar to certain varieties of hops. Clary sage is another highly unique sage that has been used in drinks for centuries. It imparts a flavor similar to muscatel and has been used to flavor wine, vermouth, and liqueurs. The essential oils in clary sage are linalyl acetate, linalool, and alpha-terpineol. One variety in Israel even has a substantial amount of geraniol. All of these compounds are common in hops. It's no wonder that beer-making took to hops, given their chemical similarity to traditional herbs like sage.

We should note that plants commonly called "sagewort" or "sagebrush" are not in the *Salvia* genus. Most are an *Artemisia*, the same genus as wormwood, and can be toxic. These plants grow in the American southwest and were historically used in culinary, medicinal, and ritual applications. One interesting similarity between *Salvia* and *Artemisia* is the presence of thujone—the chemical that got wormwood products like absinthe effectively banned in the United States. Sage contains thujone in much smaller quantities, and is much less bitter than many *Artemisia* plants. It is generally regarded as safe, although in moderate quantities.

HARVESTING

Sage is one of our hardier garden herbs at the brewery, usually making it through the first frost and sometimes even into the winter, though in a much reduced form. We often leave it in the garden as opposed to harvesting before the first frost. In general, its aroma is best preserved if harvested throughout the summer, with one final cutting before the first frost. Sage does just fine when preserved by drying. In its dried state we also notice it gives off more of its hop-like aromas. We like to use it dried in the winter; try it fresh and dried for different effects.

BREWING

Sage is powerfully aromatic—probably the reason it has been used in beer for centuries. We recommend using a small to moderate amount first, then adjusting to your liking.

Sage can also be used at any part of the process to infuse flavor: during the boil, as a flameout addition, or in the fermenter. We often add it with other herbs and plants as a bittering addition, and at flameout as an aroma addition. Sage ale in Britain was often brewed with a complement of other herbs, like betony, squinancywort, and fennel seeds. The potential combinations are endless, and sage works well with any number of garden herbs. Our recipe for a saison pairs it with lemon balm, an herb with a tea-like lemon quality.

Sage is also more soluble in alcohol, so adding it to the fermenter will actually give you a more complete aroma extraction after the yeast has generated alcohol. This is also a plant that can be enhanced by making an alcoholic tincture and adding the infusion later—either in the fermenter or before bottling.

SAGE-LEMON BALM SAISON

Batch Size: 5 gallons

OG: 1.054

FG: 1.007

ABV: 6.0%

Bitterness: 20 IBU

GRAINS
9 pounds Pilsner
4 ounces Special B
1 ounce cane sugar

MASH
Mash in with 4 gallons water to hit
147 degrees Fahrenheit
Sparge with 7½ gallons at 168 degrees
Fahrenheit

HOPS
½ ounce Citra at 60 minutes

ADDITIONAL INGREDIENTS
1 tablespoon crushed spicebush
berries (you can substitute black
peppercorns or allspice berries, or
both) at 45 minutes
½ ounce fresh lemon balm at 5 minutes
½ ounce dried sage added to the
fermenter

LENGTH OF BOIL
90 minutes with 15-minute whirlpool at
flameout

YEAST
Belgian Saison

FERMENTATION
*Pitch at 70 degrees Fahrenheit and
hold for two days, then increase to
85 degrees or higher until fermentation is complete.*

*Add the dried sage after primary fermen-
tation. Taste in one day and bottle or keg
when it reaches the desired flavor.*

SPRING

As the days get longer and temperatures rise, plants and animals awaken. Sap makes its way up from the roots of trees through the trunk, and buds start to swell. Shoots begin to emerge from the ground, drawing nourishment from the debris collected the preceding fall. All beings revel in the longer, warmer days.

Start seeds in a warm space and begin to plant them in the garden. Tap trees for sap, and gather burgeoning shoots and buds as the leaves slowly open. Spring thunderstorms knock leafy branches down that you can collect for future brew days. Wild greens that grow in early spring are in the least bitter and most tender period of their lives. And with the thawing of the ground and warm rains come the early spring mushrooms.

WHAT TO LOOK FOR:

Sap: Maple, Birch, Box Elder

Green Leaves: Sassafras, Beech, Birch, Oak, Hickory

Shoots: Blackberry Bramble, Wild Grape, Rhubarb

Sprouting Greens: Dock, Clovers, Dandelion, Lamb's Quarter, Thistle, Henbit, Chick Weed, Chicory, Polk Greens, Stinging Nettle, Sorrel

Fruits: Apricot, Strawberries

Mushrooms: Morel, Chicken of the Woods, Black Trumpet, Old Man of the Woods

Flowers: Dandelion, Honeysuckle, Apple Blossom, White Clover, Locust

Farm and Market: Beet, Arugula, Kale, Lettuces, Radish, Mint

SUGAR MAPLE

"Passing beneath some maples this after-noon, we observed several with small icicles hanging from their lower branches, although there was neither ice nor snow on the adjoining trees; we broke one off, and it proved to be congealed sap, which had exuded from the branch and frozen there during the night; natural sugar candy, as it were, growing on the tree."

—Susan Fenimore Cooper, *Rural Hours*

Collecting maple sap is one of the rites of early spring, signaling the approaching joy of warm weather. There is no sound quite like the soft symphony of sap dropping into buckets in a grove of maples.

For areas of the United States where maples are plentiful, "maple sugaring" was historically more than a rite of spring; it was the time when families made all the sugar they'd use throughout the entire year. The writer and editor Susan Fenimore Cooper (daughter of American novelist James Feni-more Cooper) described the annual sugaring of families around her family's plot of land in upstate New York. Mid-nineteenth century farms and farmers in the Empire State pro-duced hundreds of thousands of pounds of maple sugar for trade, some generating two or three thousand pounds by themselves. Fenimore Cooper noted that the farmers there were so dependent on sugar produced this time of year that they would keep "only a little white sugar for sickness; it is said that children have grown up in this county without tasting any but maple sugar."

Sugar Maple, Birch, and Box Elder are three trees that can be tapped in succession in spring here in southern Illinois. Advice on brewing with maple sap can be used for any of these trees, each of which has its own unique sap flavor profile.

Aside from their sap, the other parts of trees have enormous potential for flavor, aroma, and bittering—and sugar maples are no exception. Bark, branches, leaves, and even the buds of the maple can impart distinct flavors and aromas. In fact, a syrup made with toasted maple bark could almost be mistaken for maple syrup, in large part because the flavor of the sap is found in much of the rest of the tree. And why should this be a surprise? *This* is the distinctive taste of maple. You don't have to worry about toxicity in sugar maples, but it is important to be aware of toxicity in other trees. For instance, wild cherry bark can also be made into a syrup and the cherry fruit is edible. However, cherry pits contain cyanide, and so do the leaves.

HARVESTING

Sap

When the trees are flowing fastest, a tap will yield 3 to 5 gallons of sap in 24 hours. Thirty taps give us enough sap to entirely replace water in a 62-gallon batch of beer. We got our hands on used 55-gallon, food-grade plastic barrels where we can keep the sap until use. We dump our buckets into the barrels in the back of Aaron's pick up truck and transport it to the brewery where we store it in the walk-in until use. This involves lots of bailing into and out of barrels with cheap, 5-gallon buckets, making the roughly 440-pound barrel transportable. Fortunately, on a home brew scale, about two buckets will do for an all-grain batch, and one bucket will work for extract.

Maple sap has antimicrobial properties that naturally preserve it. However, it will begin to ferment if left at room temperature or denatured with water or other liquids like rain. If you're not going to use it immediately, store it in a refrigerated space; it will keep for up to a week. Once the sap starts to look cloudy, it is going bad.

In southern Illinois we tap trees roughly from mid-February through the beginning of March. The timing is right when the weather is freezing at night and above freezing in the day. Tap on the first warm day of a string of warm days.

On its own, maple sap tastes mildly sweet with a light minerality. To illustrate just how much we have to reduce sap to make the sweet syrup we pour over pancakes, know that it takes about 35 to 40 gallons of sap to produce one single gallon of syrup. Trees in the same grove also vary quite a bit in the volume of sap they produce. Installing three or four taps will ensure that you collect enough at once.

Bark

Maple bark has a distinctive maple character that can add maple aroma to your beer even better than syrup can. For a 5-gallon batch, cut off about a half a pound of maple bark. Only pull bark that is already loose on the tree, and only toast the bark when you're ready to brew; otherwise you risk losing the distinctive aroma.

Leaves and Branches

Maples are unmistakably brilliant in the fall, which is also the best time to harvest their leaves as they settle on the ground. We also use green leaves throughout the year, as well as branches from fallen trees.

BREWING

Sap

Sap will most definitely add extra sugar to your beer. The sugar content will vary from week to week, season to season, tree to tree, and climate to climate—a whole host of variables. You might not know exactly what the density of sugar in solution is on your brew day, but you can make a rough estimate. Assume the density of the sap is about 40 to 1, meaning you would expect 1 gallon of syrup for every 40 gallons of sap.

Bark

Maple bark flavor benefits from a long boil, so add it at the beginning of a 60-minute boil. Toast it first in a 350-degree oven for about 40 minutes, until it starts to get very aromatic. You can also boil the bark in water and save

CALCULATING MAPLE SAP'S SUGAR CONTENT

You can calculate how much sugar is in maple sap by doing the following calculation: Divide the total gallons of sap you use by 40 (for all-grain brewers, this means both mash and sparge liquid; for extract brewers, this means the liquid the extract is dissolved into). This will give you an estimate of the amount of syrup you would have had if you had boiled that sap to traditional syrup. Most beer calculation programs have maple syrup as an option and they take into account the fermentability of the sugar in maple syrup. You can therefore add that volume of maple syrup to your recipe and see how it changes your gravity. If you don't use a beer calculation program or want to know the sugar content more specifically, you can convert the volume of syrup to a rough weight of sugar. Maple syrup is 68 percent sugar. One gallon of maple syrup weighs 11 pounds, so 68 percent of 11 pounds is 7½ pounds of sugar per gallon.

We have found that maple sap imparts a good deal of mineral flavor to the beer, as well as light cherry aromas. We therefore brew our maple beers with stronger alcohol contents,

and, knowing how much the sugar content can vary, we aren't concerned too much with the exact amount of sugar in our sap. We expect the gravity to be higher in those beers, and prepare to pitch a little extra yeast to get the fermentation going.

The nice thing about sap is that you can treat it exactly like you would treat water in the brewing process. Heat it up in a hot liquor tank to mash in and sparge, or dissolve extract right into it. We usually add salts to change the water chemistry of our beers, but since we don't know the exact chemistry of our sap, we don't do that in this case. However, we know that the mineral character is pronounced in the finished product, so we usually brew beers like stouts, Baltic porters, dark strong Belgian-style beers, and beers fermented with British or Belgian yeast strains that emphasize cherry esters. In our experience, lighter beers are not as successful and tend to express less palatable rocky and green apple flavors (which is perhaps not surprising since that is what one often finds when fermenting an overabundance of sugar).

the water to infuse into a batch of beer later. Or you can make a simple syrup (in a 1:1 water-to-sugar ratio) to prime your beer or to add to your wort later to boost the sugar content.

Branches and Leaves

Branches and leaves impart different flavors, aromas, and levels of bitterness depending on whether they're collected alive or dead. A green branch taken from a tree in the

spring will drip sap and have a pronounced bitterness laced with tannins, and tastes not unlike tilled soil and fresh grass. Branches from a felled tree or leaves that have fallen to the ground have a more tannic, papery quality that tastes great in a crisp, clean, moderately bitter beer like an altbier (people have described the flavor as akin to what one smells jumping into a dried leaf pile). Fresh branches also go a long way. One 12-inch branch added to the boil at 60 minutes is plenty to give a green tannic bitterness. A quarter pound of live or dead leaves in a 5-gallon batch will also suffice to impart a hint of flavor without crowding out other aromas.

TAPPING A MAPLE TREE

EQUIPMENT

$7/16$-inch stainless steel spile

5-gallon bucket

Maple trees have to be at least 10 inches in diameter to tap once, and you can add one additional tap for every 8 inches of diameter above 10 inches, with up to four taps per tree.

Find a nice big root above the ground; the sap will be flowing from the roots up to the branches. Insert the spile into the tree somewhere between the root and a lower branch, about two feet high. You may need a drill to get the spile started. It should not go in more than about two and a half inches. A hammer may help insert the spile into the hole, but don't hit it too hard. Hook the bucket over the spile so the sap collects inside of it. (Some spiles have hooks for this purpose.) You can use any container to collect the sap—galvanized steel and plastic buckets work great, but plastic milk cartons can serve as well. Glass containers aren't appropriate because the sap could freeze and break them.

If the temperature is high, check the buckets twice a day, as the sap should be flowing vigorously. Bugs will start to come out later in the season, so keep an eye out. (Although since beer is boiled, a couple of flies and spiders in your sap won't hurt your finished product.) Exchange an empty bucket with a full one or pour your bucket into another container to transport back to your brewing area.

MAPLE PORTER

Batch Size: 5 gallons

OG: 1.067

FG: 1.014

ABV: 7.0%

Bitterness: 28 IBU

GRAINS

10 pounds 8 ounces Maris Otter

1 pound 4 ounces crystal 80°L

1 pound 4 ounces chocolate malt

MASH

Mash in with 5 gallons of maple sap to hit 150 degrees Fahrenheit

Sparge with 7 gallons of maple sap at 168 degrees Fahrenheit

HOPS

1 ounce Chinook at 60 minutes

ADDITIONAL INGREDIENTS

½ pound toasted maple bark at 60 minutes

LENGTH OF BOIL

90 minutes with 15-minute whirlpool at flameout

YEAST

British Ale

FERMENTATION

Ferment at 68 degrees Fahrenheit until primary fermentation is almost complete, then raise above 70 degrees until finished.

DANDELION

If you've never foraged for a wild plant before, there's no better place to start than dandelion. This ubiquitous non-toxic weed can be found in just about every green area, from lawns to parks to traffic medians. (Not that we advocate harvesting them from all of these locations; it's best to stay clear from places with heavy metals or car traffic.) It's one wild-growing plant that almost everyone has seen and can identify. And it has an absolute wealth of resources for the brewer.

Dandelion greens are filled with vitamin A, calcium, and potassium, and they have a bitter flavor similar to arugula. When young, they are an excellent substitute for arugula and make a nice addition to sandwiches, salads, and pizzas. Their bitterness also makes them an ideal plant to use as a bittering agent in beer.

The root of the dandelion is also bitter, though we recommend using the whole plant—stem, leaf, and root—to bitter beer. The roots have also historically been used as a coffee substitute. We use them often in stouts or other darker beers and find that these roasted roots will even add extra bitterness, just like roasted barley would.

Finally, dandelion flowers have been prized in home wine-making. Their bright, sunny floral quality gives the flowers a unique aroma, almost akin to sticking your nose in pollen. Since they're an early spring bloomer, they seem to radiate sun and warmth and make an excellent aroma addition to beer.

HARVESTING

Leaves and Roots

For bittering beer it's best to harvest the whole plant, digging deep to pull up the plant by its roots. (Of course if you want to save the plant for harvesting leaves to eat, leave the root in tact and just pull leaves as needed.) The bigger the roots, the better; they give you more bitterness with less work. If you're after larger roots specifically, you'll want a plant that's been in the ground for a couple of seasons. You may not know where those are the first year, but if you keep an eye on patches of lawn, you'll start to identify spots.

Dandelions start to appear as soon as the weather stays above freezing. You can harvest early on, but if you wait until flowers appear, you can use a larger plant that has larger leaves and more bitterness.

Flowers

Marika's Swedish grandmother, who would only be caught drinking a touch of sherry before dinner, saved a little purple book on home wine-making with a highlighted recipe for dandelion wine. No evidence exists of her home wine-making days except for this telltale volume that was found hidden behind a handful of church cookbooks after she died.

Dandelion wine is made with the blossoms of the plant, other aromatics, sugar, and water, and aged for at least a year. But the blossoms are equally good in beer—and it doesn't need to be aged for nearly as long as dandelion wine. The only problem with dandelion blossoms, as any home wine-maker will attest, is that you need a whole lot of flowers to create a pronounced aroma in the finished product. Ideally, one would collect about a gallon of blossoms per gallon of beer. If you don't have half a town helping you, though, even a quart or a pint per gallon will impart a pleasant, light floral character. Be sure to pull the yellow petals off of the green calyx, which is quite bitter. Of course, since beer is already bitter, this isn't as much of an imperative as it is for wine makers, but the more green you can take off the flower, the better. You can freeze dandelion flowers if you'd like to collect them over time. Put them in a freezer bag or vacuum seal them, and place in a freezer as soon as possible before they start to turn brown and wilt.

BREWING

Whole plant

Dandelions can replace hops entirely for low to moderately bitter beers up to about 25 IBUs. Use about a pound of plants per 5 gallons of beer. Dandelions do convey a kind of "green" flavor that's hard to describe except to say that it tastes "plant-like," almost spinach-y. Be prepared for something that tastes a little different from a floral hop, even if you're using it as a bittering ingredient, rather than a flavor or aroma addition.

You can counter this "green" flavor in several ways. You can either add hops or other flavoring and aroma ingredients at the end of the boil to cover it up (or meld with it), or you can make a maltier beer whose emphasis is on grains. Either of these strategies will cover up much of the vegetal flavors if you don't prefer them. On the other hand, you can embrace this unique flavor. We've done a Dandelion Tonic bittered with the whole plant and no hops, using the flowers as an aroma addition at the end of the boil. We also do a Spring Tonic in which we blend the dandelion in with a handful of other spring herbs and plants (for that recipe, see the chapter on stinging nettle, page 46). Letting the brew go slightly sour lends the beer a pleasant, refreshing quality and a kind of extra perceived bitterness that gives the dandelion flavor another dimension. Add a pound of dandelion greens and roots—fresh out of the ground and cleaned of dirt—at 60 minutes in a mesh bag for the full bittering effect.

Flowers

Dandelion flowers have a delicate aroma and it is best to add them at flameout or directly to the fermenter. If adding to the fermenter in a beer where the main bittering component is dandelion, you may consider a hop addition either for bittering at 60 minutes or around 30 minutes to help preserve the beer against souring. Few things have the same antimicrobial effect as hops, so it is possible that your beer will go sour if you introduce something to the fermenter in a beer that doesn't have hops. Or, just embrace the sour!

Roots Only

As we mentioned above, dandelion roots have been used as a coffee substitute for a long time. To roast dandelion roots, wash off as much dirt as possible after harvesting, and then allow it to dry or put it into a dehydrator. When thoroughly dry, put it into an oven at 350 degrees Fahrenheit and roast for 30 minutes or longer, depending on your preferred darkness. When done roasting, chop it in a food processor first, then in a coffee grinder. You can then add the grinds directly to the fermenter, or you can make a dandelion root espresso, French press, or even a cold toddy and add them to the beer in the fermenter. As with a coffee addition, it shouldn't take more than 24 hours before the flavors have sufficiently melded and the beer is ready for bottling or kegging, so wait until your fermentation is complete before adding.

DANDELION TONIC

Batch Size: 5 gallons
OG: 1.059
FG: 1.011
ABV: 6.3%
Bitterness: ? IBU

GRAINS
5 pounds 10 ounces Vienna
4 pounds 10 ounces Pilsner
15 ounces Munich

MASH
Mash in with 4½ gallons water to hit
    147 degrees Fahrenheit
Sparge with 7 gallons water at
    168 degrees Fahrenheit

HOPS
None

ADDITIONAL INGREDIENTS
1 pound dandelion greens and roots
    (whole plant) at 60 minutes
8 ounces dandelion flowers at flameout

LENGTH OF BOIL
90 minutes with 15-minute whirlpool at
    flameout

YEAST
British Ale

FERMENTATION
*Ferment at 66 degrees Fahrenheit, then
allow to rise naturally until complete.*

ROASTED DANDELION ROOT STOUT

Batch Size: 5 gallons

OG: 1.073

FG: 1.017

ABV: 7.4%

Bitterness: 43 IBU

GRAINS

11 pounds Maris Otter
1 pound roasted barley
1 pound Victory
1 pound Munich
12 ounces Special B
8 ounces flaked barley
8 ounces chocolate malt

MASH

Mash in with 4½ gallons water to hit
147 degrees Fahrenheit
Sparge with 7 gallons water at
168 degrees Fahrenheit

HOPS

1 ounce Nugget at 60 minutes
1 ounce East Kent Goldings at
15 minutes

ADDITIONAL INGREDIENTS

3 ounces roasted dandelion roots,
ground into powder and made into
espresso (or steeped in boiling
water), then added to fermenter

LENGTH OF BOIL

60 minutes with 15-minute whirlpool at
flameout

YEAST

Irish Ale

FERMENTATION

Ferment at 66 degrees Fahrenheit, then allow to rise a couple degrees each day until complete.

Add the dandelion espresso mixture and condition for one to two days.

STINGING NETTLE

Anything that stings is an unlikely choice to consume in any form—or, for that matter, to rub on one's skin. But these are all traditional uses of stinging nettle, a wild green that also has a long brewing history in England. Medicinally, it has been used as a blood purifier, a diuretic, as a central nervous system depressant, an antibacterial, and a ward against scurvy and gout. In fact "urtification" was the term given to the act of flogging with nettles to alleviate the pain of rheumatism and muscle weakness (the word is from the the nettle genus' Latin name, *Urtica*, derived from the word "to burn"). As Maude Grieve describes with irony in her classic *A Modern Herbal*, "it is a strange fact that the juice of the Nettle proves an antidote for its own sting, and being applied will afford instant relief."

Stinging nettle is one of the first plants to emerge in the woods in early spring and can cover a forest floor by late summer. Ryan, our resident trail runner, has had many occasions of discovering a patch of nettle when suddenly feeling the burning sensation of it clinging to his legs on a long run. By August or September, a patch of nettle like the one we often harvest from can be so vast that it will cover a quarter-mile radius of valleys and ridges.

For a forager, nettle offers an incredible variety of vitamins and minerals for health. Plus, it is found for such a large portion of the year that the combination of plants that

grow in concert with it make for an exciting array of very different brewing possibilities. In England, nettles were brewed into a tonic with other plants like dandelion, cleavers, burdock, meadowsweet, avens, and horehound. In late summer we find nettle in southern Illinois growing at the foot of spicebush trees, whose red berries are abundant at that time of year. The unmistakable aroma of pepper, allspice, and citrus fills the air and makes a fantastic accompaniment to nettle in a traditional English pale ale.

We include two recipes here for nettle beers brewed at two different times of the year to show how versatile this plant can be. The Spring Tonic is a beer we brew in early spring as the young, green leaves are just emerging, combining nettle as it was in England with other early spring plants—dandelion, cleavers—and a touch of ginger (as Maude Grieve advises from the recipes of English cottagers). This beer, brewed without the addition of hops, may naturally go sour. In our experience, if your brewing equipment is otherwise clean and sanitized, this should be a crisp, tart sourness caused by *Lactobacillus*, and it is a delicious drink, sour or not.

The second beer is a late summer concoction inspired by the aromas of spicebush and the tradition of English brewing. We brew an old world pale ale with nettles for bittering, spicebush branches for flavoring,

and ground spicebush berries and hops for aroma. It is a refreshing beer with a mild, herbal bitterness and a peppery finish.

HARVESTING

Gloves are an absolute must when harvesting nettles. You will quickly feel the pinprick of formic acid on your skin without them; this burning sensation can last several days. Nettles should come up easily by the root, and you can transport them to your brew house in a 5-gallon bucket. They should be used promptly after picking, within several hours at room temperature, or within 24 hours if they can be kept in a refrigerated area.

BREWING

For brewing, nettles need no preparation save for a rinse under water to get most of the dirt off the root. Place them in a large hop bag and boil for 60 minutes. Like dandelion greens, use 1 pound of nettles per 5-gallon batch for bittering. Nettles have a spinach-like flavor and a mild bitterness when compared to hops and even to dandelions. Their addition will give you a more pronounced "green" flavor reminiscent of earth and plants. Boiling nettles destroys the stinging effect. At the end of your boil the nettles will be perfectly safe to handle without gloves.

SPRING TONIC

Batch Size: 5 gallons
OG: 1.047
FG: 1.007
ABV: 5.2%
Bitterness: ? IBU

GRAINS
4 pounds Vienna
3 pounds Pilsner
2 pounds Munich

MASH
Mash in with 4 gallons water to hit
147 degrees Fahrenheit
Sparge with 7½ gallons water at
168 degrees Fahrenheit

HOPS
None

ADDITIONAL INGREDIENTS
½ pound ginger, chopped, at
60 minutes
½ pound dandelion greens and roots at
60 minutes

½ pound nettle at 30 minutes (also
feel free to add any combination of
cleavers, dock, arugula greens, or
other plants coming up in your area
in spring)

LENGTH OF BOIL
90 minutes with 15-minute whirlpool at
flameout

YEAST
American Ale

FERMENTATION
*Ferment at 66 degrees Fahrenheit, and
allow to rise naturally until fermentation is complete.*

NETTLE-SPICEBUSH ALE

Batch Size: 5 gallons
OG: 1.052
FG: 1.011
ABV: 5.4%
Bitterness: 23 IBU

GRAINS
9 pounds 12 ounces Maris Otter
6 ounces crystal 80°L

MASH
Mash in with 4 gallons water to hit
150 degrees Fahrenheit
Sparge with 6½ gallons water at
168 degrees Fahrenheit

HOPS
½ ounce Chinook at 60 minutes

ADDITIONAL INGREDIENTS
1 pound nettle at 60 minutes
2 (12-inch-long) spicebush twigs,
1 quart of spicebush leaves,
1 teaspoon spicebush berries at
60 minutes

LENGTH OF BOIL
60 minutes with 15-minute whirlpool at
flameout

YEAST
British Ale

FERMENTATION
*Ferment at 67 degrees Fahrenheit until
fermentation is nearly complete, then
raise above 70 degrees until complete.*

JAPANESE HONEYSUCKLE

As with dandelion, chances are pretty high that you have already encountered Japanese honeysuckle. That's because it is a plant that has a tendency to take over its environment, and its aroma is arresting. On a sunny spring day, while walking down a sidewalk or even driving in a car, you will suddenly be bowled over by the powerful smell of honey and tropical fruit probably before you even register honeysuckle plants in the vicinity.

Japanese honeysuckle is not native to the United States and can be considered a noxious weed. It competes for root space with, and can crowd out light to, other native plants. In some warmer parts of the southern United States it is even a semi-evergreen plant, making it hardier than other native species. In short, while its aroma is beguiling, it can be a gigantic nuisance.

However, in Japan this honeysuckle has also been used traditionally as a tea to treat a bevy of ailments: bacterial dysentery, enteritis, laryngitis, colds, fevers, flus—it is even used topically for sores, boils, and scabies! It's no wonder honeysuckle seems to work miracles for health: the plant has at least a dozen antiviral compounds. Botanist James Duke suggests that while we consider Japanese honeysuckle a serious weed, it "might be managed by using it for proven medicinal purposes."

For beer, however, Japanese honeysuckle has an even greater benefit: it can give the aroma of honey in a way that honey very often cannot. The irony, of course, with using honey in beer is that it is almost entirely fermentable. Stir a gallon of fresh wildflower honey into your boiling wort, and a couple weeks later when fermentation is complete, you'll be left wondering where it all went. Honeysuckle, however, provides the nectar we wish we could get from honey itself; it's a sweet, rich, often passion fruit-like floral aroma that can complement a huge variety of hops and yeast strains.

HARVESTING

Honeysuckle is a mid-spring bloomer that reaches its peak in size and aromatic potential toward the end of May for us in southern Illinois (although it can bloom even into October, particularly in warmer climates). Japanese honeysuckle can be distinguished from other varieties by noting the smooth (not serrated), ovular leaves, and the flowers that turn from white or pink to yellow before they die. Large white or yellow trumpet-shaped flowers that seem to be bursting from the seams are prime for picking. In addition, because they are so aromatic, you can do more with fewer flowers than you can with other blooms that are smaller or slightly less pungent.

Ideally, it's best to pick the flowers as close as possible to the time you will be adding them to your beer to preserve the bountiful aromatics. If harvesting on a brew day, harvest while mashing or boiling your wort. If it's not possible to harvest and pitch fresh flowers, you can also dry the flowers and add them on a later date. In fact, you can always buy dried honeysuckle flowers from Asian grocery stores or teashops if the flowers are slightly out of season, or if you don't have a honeysuckle patch near you.

BREWING

Honeysuckle is powerful and a little goes a long way. The character it adds to beer also changes depending on the quantity you add. A small amount—which is what we prefer—in combination with a robust Belgian yeast strain carries beautiful peach, honey, and lightly tropical aromas. In greater quantities, you will find more floral character and a stronger honey punch. Use too much and the beer can verge to medicinal chalky territory. This is a great flower to experiment with because you can harvest enough for a batch of beer during downtime while brewing and because patches of honeysuckle grow like, well, weeds. Plop yourself in front of a bush and start picking, and you'll have enough flowers in less than an hour. If using dried blossoms, use about a third of the amount of flowers you would normally use fresh. We use about 5 ounces of flowers, added at flameout.

LOVE IT, HATE IT, LIVE WITH IT

We often find ourselves in a love-hate relationship with invasive species like Japanese
honeysuckle. We don't want it to crowd out
our native plants, and yet there's something
so special about its flavor, aroma, and even its
medicinal properties that keep us from want-
ing to eradicate it completely. Fortunately with
some diligent management of our environment, we can preserve some invasive species
while maintaining plants that are native to our
region.

The Plant Conservation Alliance (PCA) is a
consortium of 10 federal government member
agencies as well as hundreds of experts in
various disciplines within the field of conservation. PCA provides money for research,
conservation, restoration, and outreach in
order to solve problems precisely like that
of Japanese honeysuckle. PCA also creates
fact sheets on invasive species and provides
detailed information about how to contain
plants using manual, mechanical, chemical,
and biological options. Its website www
.nps.gov/plants is a great resource for those
interested in how to maintain their gardens,
backyards, and the wild spaces around them.

HONEYSUCKLE BLONDE

Batch Size: 5 gallons

OG: 1.052

FG: 1.008

ABV: 5.7%

Bitterness: 25 IBU

GRAINS

5 pounds 12 ounces Pilsner

3 pounds 4 ounces Vienna

10 ounces crystal 10°L (or biscuit malt)

6 ounces Special B

MASH

Mash in with 4 gallons water to hit 149 degrees Fahrenheit

Sparge with 7½ gallons water at 168 degrees Fahrenheit

HOPS

½ ounce Citra at 60 minutes

ADDITIONAL INGREDIENTS

5 ounces fresh honeysuckle flowers at flameout

LENGTH OF BOIL

90 minutes with 15-minute whirlpool at flameout

YEAST

Belgian Abbey Ale

FERMENTATION

Ferment at 67 degrees Fahrenheit for first three days, then allow to rise naturally above 70 degrees until complete.

ARUGULA

Arugula is among the first greens that pop up in the spring. Bitter, peppery, spicy, we use it on pizzas at the brewery on the weekends, and it provides several extra ways to punch up a beer.

The history of arugula stretches back to pre-medieval Europe and the Mediterranean. Its leaves were used in salads even back then, and its seeds were eaten as an aphrodisiac. Today it's grown all over the United States and in many parts of the world. Although bitter, it is a beloved green with a uniquely peppery bite that adds dimension to any dish.

We use the leaves and roots of the plant in ways not dissimilar to dandelion. The leaves are great for bittering and can add an extra peppery flavor, while the root can be roasted and added to the fermenter for a lightly spicy toasted or chocolate flavor. The seeds are a dimension we haven't explored too much yet, and require a little patience on the part of the gardener or farmer. Instead of eating the whole plant, let it go to seed and harvest the seeds later in the season. Toasted very lightly, we would expect them to give a slightly peppery, nutty flavor.

HARVESTING

For brewing, it's often more advantageous to use a plant after it's beyond its ideal stage for eating. This couldn't be more true of arugula. Whereas it's better to harvest arugula

leaves for food when they're young—before they get tough and quite bitter—it's better to harvest for beer when the plant is older. This is due to two primary factors: First, there's more bittering potential in the greens when they're older, and when they're bigger you can harvest more at once. Second, since the roots will have more time to develop, they too will be larger. When young, arugula roots may not be much larger than the tip of your pinkie finger. Older, they might fit as a bunch in the palm of your hand. If you have an arugula plant, harvest as much of the young leaves as you can to eat first, then let the plant go to seed and use what's left in beer. If you buy your arugula from a farmer or belong to a CSA, ask them if they can sell you what's left at the end of their harvest. Often this plant will just be composted anyway.

BREWING

Leaves

Use the leaves as a bittering addition in place of hops. They don't seem to be quite as bitter as dandelion in our experience, so we've substituted half the hops for arugula leaves. When calculating your recipe, figure your hop addition at half the IBUs it would normally be and then substitute the rest at ½ to 1 pound of arugula leaves per 5 gallons of beer. This works well for beers between 15 and 25 IBU. Higher than this you

taste from plant to plant and at different roasting temperatures. It's all a bit like roasting coffee. A lighter roast will often help bring out more of the *terroir* of a bean, since your palate doesn't have to pick through the denser, chewier roasted qualities, making it easier to tell the difference in profiles from bean to bean. Plants seem to act similarly. Lightly roasted arugula root in some ways helps bring out the earthy spice that's unique to the plant. It's toasty, has hints of chocolate, but retains a nuttiness and pepper you can't get solely from the leaves. Try toasting the root in an oven at 325 degrees Fahrenheit until it starts to turn a light-to-medium brown tone, about 15 to 20 minutes.

When the roots are only lightly roasted, it's a bit tricky to grind them and add them to a beer. Darker roasts help the physical compound break down so it's easier to grind like a coffee. Grinding the roots just helps to add surface area and help the flavor disperse into your beer. Try to chop the roots into smaller pieces with a knife first and then add to a food processor.

When you have a fairly finely chopped product you can either add it directly to the fermenter (in a sanitized mesh bag) or straight to the beer at the end of fermentation; or you can actually make a "coffee" with the roots using a percolator or French press. Any of these methods will work, and with such a light roast you shouldn't get too much acrid bitterness when making a hot tincture in a percolator or French press, as opposed to a "cold press" tincture or addition straight to the fermenter.

would probably want to double the arugula addition—if you can fit it into your kettle! In general these leaves are less bitter than hops so better for beers with lower IBUs. Put the leaves into a mesh bag and add to the boil.

Roots

We roast a lot of roots at the brewery. You would be amazed at how varied they can

ARUGULA RYE PORTER

Batch Size: 5 gallons

OG: 1.053

FG: 1.011

ABV: 5.4%

Bitterness: 31 IBU

GRAINS
6 pounds 8 ounces Maris Otter
1 pound 8 ounces rye
1 pound 2 ounces crystal 80°L
1 pound chocolate malt
8 ounces flaked wheat

MASH
Mash in with 4½ gallons water to hit
149 degrees Fahrenheit
Sparge with 6 gallons water at
168 degrees Fahrenheit

HOPS
½ ounce Nugget at 60 minutes

ADDITIONAL INGREDIENTS
½ pound arugula leaves at 60 minutes
½ cup arugula root, toasted and ground,
added to the fermenter

LENGTH OF BOIL
60 minutes with 15-minute whirlpool at
flameout

YEAST
British Ale

FERMENTATION
*Ferment at 67 degrees Fahrenheit until
fermentation is nearly complete, then
allow to rise naturally above 70 degrees
until complete.*

*Boil the ground arugula root in ½ cup
of water for 3 minutes. Allow to cool
slightly, then pour the arugula root
water mixture into the fermenter at the
end of fermentation. You may start by
adding half the mixture, then tasting
the beer and adding more to suit your
taste.*

RHUBARB

Rhubarb deserves a special mention not for its versatility in brewing—only the stalks are edible—but because it is one of the first signs of life that springs from the garden in April. Also known as pie plant for the dish in which we very often find it, rhubarb is the classic tart edible that adds a green-apple-like bite.

Rhubarb is also the kind of plant that you tend to have way more of than you know what to do with. The 1904 *Encyclopedia of American Horticulture* opines that 10 to 20 plants will supply the needs of one household. But as many gardeners know, a fully mature rhubarb plant can have dozens of big viable stalks per plant, so unless you're feeding an army of rhubarb-mad children, you'd likely have quite a bit to spare working under those guidelines.

Fortunately, you need to add a lot of rhubarb to beer to really taste the sharp malic acid in the stalks. It's a great way to get rid of a bumper crop or an abundance of stalks from your local CSA. It also has the benefit of adding a lemon-like finish to a beer, which should be done fermenting and ready to bottle just as you start transitioning to lighter spring and summer drinking fare.

HARVESTING
Rhubarb stalks can be found all over farmers' markets and in grocery stores by early spring, and should already be cleaned of

the leaves. If you're doing the harvesting, pull the stalk from the ground at the base and trim off the green leaf. Harvest about a third to a half of the stalks on each plant to provide enough green cover for the plant.

The leaf contains oxalic acid, an acid that is common in some foods, but may contain other toxins and should not be eaten. The stalks, on the other hand, contain a much smaller amount of oxalic acid and are edible. Their acidity is dominated by malic acid, the sharp, tart flavor we often associate with grapes and green apples. Sometimes, however, after a late frost, oxalic acid can seep into the stalk. If you see brown or black spots or the stalks are mushy, they should be avoided.

Rhubarb stalks can be kept refrigerated for a week. If you will not use them directly after harvesting, cut them into pieces and freeze in freezer bags.

BREWING

You will taste the rhubarb more if you make a beer that is lighter in body without a lot of extra flavors in the mix. A light saison or a pale ale enhanced with Citra, Amarillo, Chinook, or other citrus-oriented hops make a great combination. You will need at least 4 pounds of rhubarb for a 5-gallon batch. Chop roughly and add to the kettle in a bag at 20 minutes before the end of the boil. The effect of boiling should also soften the acidity and allow the plant to blend in more with the yeast, or hops.

Another technique we discovered when making rhubarb soda is to cook the rhubarb down and add it to the beer in the fermenter. This seems to help break down the plant and make some of the sugars and aromas accessible. To do this, dice the rhubarb and cook it in a pot with a little bit of water so it doesn't burn. After about 45 minutes to an hour, the rhubarb will break down and look mushy and a little gray. It's not pretty, but it will add a lot of character to your beer, even a little bit of "dank funk-iness," as our soda-maker Kyle will attest. This technique makes a great addition to saisons or Brett beers. Add to the fermenter after primary fermentation is complete. It will float on top so you will have to rack below (easier for those who use glass carboys rather than plastic buckets). Taste test and rack when you like the flavor.

RHUBARB SAISON

Batch Size: 5 gallons
OG: 1.047
FG: 1.005
ABV: 5.4%
Bitterness: 22 IBU

GRAINS
5 pounds Pilsner
4 pounds Vienna

MASH
Mash in with 4 gallons water to hit
    147 degrees Fahrenheit
Sparge with 7½ gallons water at
    168 degrees Fahrenheit

HOPS
⅔ ounce Nugget at 60 minutes

ADDITIONAL INGREDIENTS
4 pounds rhubarb cooked down and
    added to the fermenter

LENGTH OF BOIL
90 minutes with 15-minute whirlpool at
    flameout

YEAST
Belgian Saison

FERMENTATION
*Ferment at 70 degrees Fahrenheit and
let rise to 85 or more degrees naturally.*

*Add the cooked rhubarb after primary
fermentation is complete. Taste test and
rack when you like the flavor.*

MINT

Like basil, mint is an herb that needs no introduction. Also like basil, it has so many variations and so much variation within the variations that you can find two spearmint plants that taste radically different from one another. But variety, of course, is the spice of life, and different varieties of mint will reward your palate. Water mint (sometimes called bergamot mint) has hints of orange and lemon, and even tastes so much like lavender that it's been called "American lavender." Pineapple mint is a sweet species of mint that is slightly tropical, while chocolate mint is actually just a black peppermint variety that tastes pretty close to an Andes chocolate. Peppermint is also one of only two species of plant that contains the chemical compound menthol (North American cornmint is the other). You may associate menthol with cigarettes, but it is a fascinating compound that actually creates the same physical effect on the human body as coldness. Ever wonder why mint sometimes actually feels cool?

That cooling factor is something we make use of in our Mumm beer. We are deeply indebted to a brilliant recipe in *The Home-brewer's Garden* for Mumm, a beer we brewed as home brewers and found intriguing. At the brewery, we tweaked the grain bill and found it a great complement to the herbs we had planted in the garden right by our front door. The recipe included is for the beer we usually brew with mint (sometimes chocolate mint), basil, lavender, rosemary, sage, and

lemon thyme. It always has a cool finish from the mint, so we make sure there's a substantial addition in every version we brew.

There are also a handful of wild "mints" that can be foraged that are in the same family (Lamiaceae) but are not of the same genus (*Mentha*) as the mints we grow in the garden. One is perilla (also called shiso), an invasive plant especially widespread in the south. Its broad green and purple leaves are like an earthy mint with a hint of basil, often used in Japanese cooking. Wild bergamot is another plant that has been used extensively by Native Americans. Its flavor varies to some degree. It can taste a bit like thyme or oregano and resembles bergamot tea and rose geranium. Other species of the *Monarda* genus, of which it is a part, have been used as thyme substitutes and as tea by the Shakers in upstate New York (Oswego tea). It is an interesting savory, minty plant.

Virginia mountain mint (*Pycnanthemum virginianum*), gray mountain mint, and hairy mountain mint are another set of similar plants in the Lamiaceae family. Virginia mountain mint has a spicy, profound mint character, and sometimes tastes like eucalyptus and pennyroyal, another similar plant. The American and European versions of pennyroyal (which are plants in two different genuses of the Lamiaceae family) have been used as teas for many years, but both contain the compound pulegone, which is an abortifacient and can be deadly in high amounts. Virginia mountain mint may also be abortive, although its concentration of pulegone is much lower than in pennyroyal, and it does not appear to have a documented history of poisoning people. We do not recommend the consumption of pennyroyal.

HARVESTING

Mint grows like a weed in our garden. Even with constant pruning it lasts through the summer and early fall, and sometimes even hangs on after the first frost. We harvest the whole plant at the end of the growing season and dry it for use in the winter.

True to its reputation, perilla has invaded our garden, particularly around the hops and at the edge of our rock wall. If you're weeding and take out a perilla plant, use the whole plant in a beer—stems, stalks, and all. And if you have some left in your garden that dries up and stays there through the winter, you can still use the dried seedpods that remain at the top of the stalk for brewing as well. They have a milder flavor than the greens, and can often blend even better into a beer. You'll be looking for the leaves of wild bergamot and Virginia mountain mint, as well as cultivated mint; these can also be harvested from spring through fall or dried at the end of the season.

BREWING

Mint gives a lot of flavor when boiled or steeped, so you can experiment with adding it at different parts of the boil. We add it at 60 minutes for the Mumm, and do an aroma addition at 10 for the stout with chocolate mint. Macerating mint with alcohol is another option, a bit like making a mojito. In fact, you can let any one of a number of different aromatics steep with the mint and then blend that into the beer later.

The same processes can be tried with the wild mint-like plants, although since each of their essential oil compositions are unique, these techniques will give different results. When in doubt, we always add plants at different points during the boil (60 minutes, 20 minutes, and flameout, for instance). You can experiment with just a 60-minute addition, just a 20-minute addition, or just a flameout addition to see how each method performs. And you can always add more of the plant to the fermenter to bump up the aroma if you don't add enough to the boil.

CHOCOLATE MINT STOUT

Batch Size: 5 gallons

OG: 1.064

FG: 1.014

ABV: 6.6%

Bitterness: 29 IBU

GRAINS
8 pounds Maris Otter
12 ounces crystal 80°L
12 ounces chocolate malt
8 ounces Munich
8 ounces roasted barley
4 ounces Special B

MASH
Mash in with 5½ gallons water to hit
    150 degrees Fahrenheit
Sparge with 5½ gallons water at
    168 degrees Fahrenheit

HOPS
½ ounce Nugget at 60 minutes

ADDITIONAL INGREDIENTS
8 fresh (8-inch-long) sprigs chocolate
    mint at 60 minutes
8 fresh (8-inch-long) sprigs chocolate
    mint at 10 minutes

LENGTH OF BOIL
60 minutes with 15-minute whirlpool at
    flameout

YEAST
British Ale

FERMENTATION
*Ferment at 67 degrees Fahrenheit until
fermentation is nearly complete, then
allow to rise naturally above 70 degrees
until complete.*

*Add more sprigs of mint to the fermenter
after primary fermentation is complete,
if desired.*

MUMM

Batch Size: 5 gallons

OG: 1.062

FG: 1.013

ABV: 6.5%

Bitterness: ? IBU

GRAINS

8 pounds Munich

5 pounds Maris Otter

3 pounds rye

8 ounces crystal 60°L

8 ounces flaked wheat

5 ounces roasted barley

4 ounces Midnight Wheat

MASH

Mash in with 5 gallons water to hit
    149 degrees Fahrenheit

Sparge with 6 gallons water at
    168 degrees Fahrenheit

HOPS

None

ADDITIONAL INGREDIENTS

2 sprigs each of half a dozen or more
    garden herbs at 60 minutes. We
    usually use mint or chocolate mint
    (sometimes both), basil, lavender,
    rosemary, sage, and lemon thyme.
    Also substitute with wild mints or any
    other herbs that grow in your area.

LENGTH OF BOIL

60 minutes with 15-minute whirlpool at
    flameout

YEAST

British Ale

FERMENTATION

*Ferment at 67 degrees Fahrenheit until
fermentation is nearly complete, then
allow to rise naturally above 70 degrees
until complete.*

SUMMER

Spring and summer have a tendency to meld together in southern Illinois. Sometimes one stretches into the other; sometimes summer just comes early. The woods are abundantly green and the mosquitoes, ticks, moths, butterflies, skinks, snakes, and other critters emerge in full force. Greens become bitterer with the rising temperatures, and plants begin to flower in abundance. This is a good time to collect bittering greens and is the best time to gather and preserve for the fall and winter. Freeze fruits and chanterelle mushrooms if you have a big harvest.

WHAT TO LOOK FOR:

Flowers: Elderflower, Daisy, Day Lily, Nasturtium, Yellow Sweet Clover, Bee Balm, Rose, Fennel

Herbs: Most Garden Herbs, Lavender, Basil, Mint, Sage, Virginia Mountain Mint, Perilla

Greens: Horseradish, Dandelion, Dock, Arugula, Turnip, Mustard, Beets

Leaves: Sassafras, Spicebush, Oak, Hickory

Wild Fruit and Berries: Blackberries, Blueberries, Raspberries, Plums, Gooseberries, Elderberries, Salmon Berry, Spicebush, Juniper,

Mushrooms: Chanterelle, Boletus (Porcini)

Seeds: Sunflower, Sumac

Nuts: Green Walnuts

Farm and Market: Carrot, Cucumber, Corn, Eggplant, Melon, Peppers, Summer Squash, Tomatoes, Tomatillos, Cherries, Peaches, Figs

CHANTERELLE

At the height of spring and summer the forest is awash with green. But a lucky traveler sauntering through thick, verdant brush, over moist ground and through a grove of white oaks, may catch flashes of color scattered like gold over the forest floor and hopefully be rewarded with a trove of chanterelle mushrooms.

Chanterelles grow abundantly in the Northern Hemisphere, usually in oak and conifer forests. They are orange-yellow and open wide into a wavy trumpet cap, reminiscent of a flower. Their gills are forked and they can grow two or three inches tall—sometimes much bigger, as in varieties like the California chanterelle (*Cantharellus californicus*) and the white chanterelle (*Cantharellus subalbidus*). They smell and taste like apricot and butter, which makes them ideal for pasta and risotto—their most natural habitat, outside of the forest.

The fruity flavor and earthy aroma of chanterelles also make them ideal for beer, particularly farmhouse ales that feature estery, often funky flavors and a crisp, dry finish that allows the mushrooms to take center stage. Our favorite beers have been saisons and bières de garde, but most importantly you should think about creating a beer with a lighter malt character and without a lot of hop aroma or bitterness in order to allow the somewhat delicate flavor of the mushroom to come through.

HARVESTING

Chanterelles are a good beginner's mushroom because of their distinct shape and color, and because of the fact that they only have a couple of dangerous but easily identifable look-alikes. The Jack-o-lantern mushroom is one such look-alike that can be distinguished by its circular (rather than wavy) cap and gills that don't fork like the true chanterelle. Jack-o-lanterns are also more orange than yellow and don't have the distinctive fruity aroma of a chanterelle.

Another species to be aware of is false chanterelle (*Hygrophoropsis aurantiaca*) which is not poisonous, but not a true chanterelle. It is generally a deeper orange color and lacks the pungent apricot aroma of the true chanterelle. Finally, there are two poisonous mushrooms in the *Cortinarius* genus that only moderately resemble chanterelles, but are very toxic, so they're worth mentioning. The Lethal webcap (*Cortinarius rubellus*) and the False webcap (*Cortinarius orellanus*) are a dark orange-brown but do not have forking gills, and turn a rusty color as they age. They don't very much resemble the golden chanterelle most people are familiar with, but do look similar to the Funnel chanterelle (*Craterellus tubaeformis*) and grow in similar areas. Consult a mushroom expert and reliable mushroom hunting books before doing any foraging for mushrooms.

Chanterelles are a classic summer mushroom that comes up around June or July in southern Illinois. To harvest, cut the mushrooms from the base so you don't have to spend as much time cleaning them later. You want to keep the air moving around them so carry them in a basket or lay them out on paper towels when you return home. Lightly brush the soil from the mushroom, although if there's still a little dirt left it won't hurt the beer.

If you find a particularly large patch of mushrooms you may be overwhelmed with riches—too many to eat and too many even for beer. We've had good success freezing and dehydrating mushrooms for beer-making. (Using frozen and dehydrated mushrooms might not be as good in cooking because the texture doesn't hold up, but for beer-making we're only interested in flavor and aroma, which are well-preserved using these methods.) Preserving mushrooms also allows you to keep them for cooler months when you may be able to make varieties of beer that ferment at lower temperatures. This is how we were able to add mushrooms to our bière de garde, which we ferment in January.

BREWING

Since they're not bitter, chanterelles are best as flavor and aroma additions. Add them like you would a whole cone hop toward the middle and end of your boil in big mesh bags. We often add plants throughout the whole boil in order to create a deeper infusion of flavor, as in the recipe for the Chanterelle Bière de Garde. A handful every 20 minutes from beginning to end, with a big infusion at the flameout will give a robust apricot flavor, slightly buttery on the finish, which complements the dry, pepper and fruit aromatics of the yeast strain. About a pound and a half of fresh mushrooms, or half a pound of dried mushrooms, will be good for a 5-gallon batch.

Randy Mosher also suggests creating a tincture with chanterelles in vodka in his book *Radical Brewing*. This method calls for adding the infusion at bottling, another way to preserve some of the delicate aromatics of the mushroom. We can attest to the effectiveness of this method, although it's not the one we use at the brewery. Aaron infused vodka with chanterelles as a home liqueur years ago and we were all amazed by the flavor and aroma—it makes for an interesting aperitif as much as it does an addition to beer.

HUNTING FOR MUSHROOMS

Want to learn more about hunting for mushrooms but don't know where to start? Many areas have mushrooms clubs, which offer a wealth of resources for the beginner: seasoned mushroom hunters, knowledgeable field guides, and organized walks through mushroom territory. Don't have a club in your area? Pick up a reliable book, like *The Complete Mushroom Hunter* or regional guides (*Mushrooms of Illinois* is one we consult frequently), and find a seasoned forager. There's no substitute for an expert who can point out subtle differences between species and teach you reliable techniques for distinguishing between poisonous and non-poisonous varieties. Farmers' markets are seeing an explosion of interest in mushrooms and can be a great place to connect with mushrooms growers, hunters, and others who can take you on walks or teach you about various species. Just don't be surprised if they keep some of their secret spots to themselves!

CHANTERELLE BIÈRE DE GARDE

Batch Size: 5 gallons

OG: 1.064

FG: 1.014

ABV: 6.5%

Bitterness: 26 IBU

GRAINS

5 pounds 10 ounces Pilsner
4 pounds 10 ounces Vienna
1 pound 5 ounces Munich
11 ounces crystal 20°L

MASH

Mash in with 4½ gallons water to hit
    147 degrees Fahrenheit
Sparge with 7 gallons water at
    168 degrees Fahrenheit

HOPS

½ ounce Columbus at 60 minutes
¾ ounce Hallertauer Mittelfrüh at
    10 minutes

ADDITIONAL INGREDIENTS

26 ounces fresh chanterelle mushrooms
3½ ounces in first wort
3½ ounces at 60 minutes
3½ ounces at 30 minutes
15½ ounces at 15 minutes

LENGTH OF BOIL

90 minutes with 15-minute whirlpool at
    flameout

YEAST

German Alt

FERMENTATION

Ferment at 58 degrees Fahrenheit for first two weeks, then allow to rise naturally above 70 degrees until complete.

BLACK TRUMPET MUSHROOM

We use two types of mushrooms regularly in our beer: Black Trumpets and Chanterelles, both of which start to cover the forest floor in June. Their flavors couldn't be more different or distinct. While chanterelles are bright and fruity, black trumpets are chocolatey and nutty with a deep, rich earthy quality.

Black trumpets and chanterelles are both in the Cantharellaceae family, whose spore-bearing undersurfaces are smooth, wrinkled, or gill-like, and are thought to form a mutually beneficial relationship with the roots of trees around which they are found. Black trumpets therefore look much like smooth chanterelles (whose gills have less pronounced ridges), with a slightly narrower trumpet shape and a dirty brown to black color. They have no poisonous look-alikes, which makes them one of the safer mushrooms to hunt; however, their dark color and leafy shape also make them a more challenging find.

HARVESTING

We generally find black trumpets growing on south- and west-facing slopes and near oak trees, often on ridgetops or areas where there's a lot of moss. Usually they aren't quite as abundant as chanterelles, although a wet late spring will bring a bounty. Like chanterelles, harvest by cutting the mushrooms at their base, above the soil, to keep yourself from cleaning dirt later.

Dehydrating seems to preserve the aroma of black trumpets well, even concentrating the flavors to pack a powerful mushroomy chocolate punch. In fact, we usually use them dehydrated, as opposed to fresh, in our beer. A typical food dehydrator will do the job, as well as a window screen with a fan set up to blow air around the mushrooms. Once dry, mushrooms can be placed into a freezer bag or mason jar and will keep for a year or two without losing very much flavor or aroma.

BREWING

Homebrewers often ask us if we're worried about putting dirt in our beer. Mushrooms, covered with dirt, often in their gills where it is difficult to extract, are exactly the kind of thing that seems worrisome.

In short, no; we aren't worried about dirt. Anything that has dirt goes into beer on the "hot side"—before it is cooled to fermentation temperatures, when bacteria can develop. Boiling is the best form of sterilization, and we always do a 15-minute whirlpool at flameout so anything added late in the boil still gets fully sanitized. The whirlpool also helps to collect any bits of dirt along with the trub in the center of the kettle so that it's not transferred to the fermenter. And any speck of dirt in the fermenter will fall out of solution with the yeast so there shouldn't be any dirt left in the finished product.

Since we brew with the mushrooms in their dehydrated form, we add them to the boil around 30 minutes, and then again just before the end of the boil, in order to give them time to rehydrate and to release their flavor and aroma. The concentrated flavors pack a wallop, and we've had good results without needing to add the mushrooms earlier in the boil. Alternatively, you can add the mushrooms directly to the fermenter by rehydrating them first in hot water, which is what we do in our Black Trumpet Milk Stout. If adding the mushrooms fresh, use about three times as many as dried. Make sure the mushrooms go into a large mesh bag as they will expand in the wort.

BLACK TRUMPET MILK STOUT

Batch Size: 5 gallons
OG: 1.052
FG: 1.013
ABV: 5.2%
Bitterness: 29 IBU

GRAINS
5 pounds 4 ounces Maris Otter
13 ounces Munich
13 ounces flaked wheat
13 ounces crystal 80°L
13 ounces chocolate malt
13 ounces roasted barley

MASH
Mash in with 4½ gallons water to hit
147 degrees Fahrenheit
Sparge with 7 gallons water at
168 degrees Fahrenheit

HOPS
¾ ounce Citra at 60 minutes

ADDITIONAL INGREDIENTS
13 ounce lactose at end of boil
1 ounce dried black trumpet
mushrooms, rehydrated and added to
the fermenter

LENGTH OF BOIL
60 minutes with 15-minute whirlpool at
flameout

YEAST
English Ale

FERMENTATION
*Ferment at 68 degrees Fahrenheit for
the first week, then allow to rise naturally above 70 degrees until complete.*

*Crush mushrooms coarsely. Bring a
pint of water to a boil and pour over
mushrooms in a mason jar. Put cling
wrap over the top of the jar and poke
a hole to let steam out. Let sit at room
temperature until cool. Pitch the entire
contents into fermenter after primary.*

AMERICAN ELDER

If any of the medicinal aspects or the folk stories about the plants in this book have intrigued you, we highly recommend you to pick up a copy of *Sacred and Herbal Healing Beers* by Stephen Harrod Buhner. His chapter on the elder plant in particular is rhapsodic, combining European mythology with explanations of traditional uses of the plant and historical recipes for beer using the flower and berry. You will understand how the elder plant has held sacred power over the forest in oral traditions, and why it has "often been likened to a complete herbal pharmacy in itself."

Southern Illinois is dazzled with elderflowers in the spring. Their bright white flowers gleam like jewels, making it easy for us to mark the places to return to in summer, when foliage is denser and the berries are hidden. Elder shrubs give us bright flowers in May which we can use to add a floral, lightly lemony, and even nutty character to beer, and drooping black berries in August that give rich, blueberry-like depth. It is no wonder that the old English-style ale, Ebulon, brewed with elderberries, has been likened to Port wine for its rich fruitiness.

Elders can also be transplanted quite well. Aaron found a promising shrub on our property and moved it outside the corner of the goat pen. Within two years the tree was 9 feet tall, with billowing flowers and berries that provided us with more than enough for several batches of beer. An elder growing wild near your property will more than likely provide enough flowers or fruit for your own brewing needs. Just remember to leave some flowers if you'd like to harvest the berries later in the season.

HARVESTING

Flowers

Elder bark, root, leaves, and unripe elderberries are toxic. Flowers and ripe berries, however, are perfectly safe to eat. To harvest the flowers, you'll want to collect them around mid-day when they are fully open. The flowers grow in clusters; you should cut the cluster where it stems from the main branch and pull off as much of the flower from the stem as possible. Use only bright white flowers—nothing that has turned brown. Brown flowers smell a little of molding lemons and can affect the flavor of an entire batch of beer, syrup, liqueur, or anything else you may make with them.

Berries

Elderberries are a prized fruit for all of the critters of the forest, so you've got to be on your game to get there first. As soon as they turn nearly black and are drooping from the weight of their liquid sweetness, they are ready to be harvested. Be careful, though, as the berries quickly go from ripe to overripe and smell like oxidized vinegar. Leave these berries behind.

As with the flowers, cut the cluster where it stems from the main branch and pull off as many of the berries as possible. We've found a quick way of doing this by freezing the clusters first, then scraping off the berries with a fork. They should drop easily into a bowl. If you have a bumper crop, the berries can be frozen for a year or more and easily added to beer later on.

BREWING

Flowers

The flowers can be used immediately in a batch of beer, or can be preserved by creating a syrup or by drying. To make a syrup you can use later to infuse into beer, stuff a mason jar full of flowers and cover with water. Let stand 48 hours, then remove the flowers. You can add sugar to this solution (a ratio of 1:1 water to sugar will make a simple syrup) or put the liquid tincture in the refrigerator for a month. To dry the flowers, lay them on a thin mesh screen and allow them to air dry. Put them in a mason jar and they will stay good for at least two years, retaining an intense nutty character. Add about ½ ounce (10 grams) of fresh flowers for a 5-gallon batch.

Berries

Use at least 6 pounds of berries for a 5-gallon batch, and ideally closer to 10 pounds. Mash lightly before adding the berries to the boil in a mesh bag. Elderberries are very astringent, so we often dial back our hop addition and allow the beer to condition for at least six months before serving.

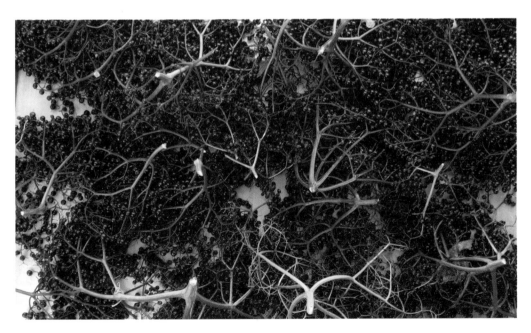

ELDERFLOWER WITBIER

Batch Size: 5 gallons
OG: 1.048
FG: 1.008
ABV: 5.3%
Bitterness: 13 IBU

GRAINS
4 pounds 8 ounces Pilsner
4 pounds 8 ounces wheat
6 ounces flaked oats

MASH
Mash in with 4 gallons water to hit
    147 degrees Fahrenheit
Sparge with 7½ gallons water at
    168 degrees Fahrenheit

HOPS
½ ounce East Kent Goldings at
    60 minutes
½ ounce Cascade at 10 minutes

ADDITIONAL INGREDIENTS
1 tablespoon coriander seed, crushed at
    5 minutes
1 cup fresh elderflower at 2 minutes

LENGTH OF BOIL
90 minutes with 15-minute whirlpool at
    flameout

YEAST
Belgian Witbier

FERMENTATION
*Ferment at 66 degrees Fahrenheit for
two days, then allow to rise about
2 degrees every day until complete.*

EBULON

Batch Size: 5 gallons

OG: 1.095–1.105 (this number will vary due to your efficiency; don't be afraid to boil longer to concentrate the sugars for a higher original gravity)

FG: 1.025

ABV: 11.7%

Bitterness: 42 IBU

GRAINS
18 pounds Maris Otter

1 pound table sugar

MASH
Mash in with 4 gallons water to hit 147 degrees Fahrenheit

Sparge with 7½ gallons water at 168 degrees Fahrenheit

HOPS
1 ounce Nugget at 60 minutes

ADDITIONAL INGREDIENTS
6 pounds ripe elderberries at 20 minutes

LENGTH OF BOIL
120 minutes with 15-minute whirlpool at flameout

YEAST
British Ale

FERMENTATION
Start at 64 degrees Fahrenheit and allow to rise to 68 degrees after five days.

To enhance the port-like character of this beer, we add toasted oak (see more about oak in that chapter, on page 150) in secondary, and let it sit for another month. Then rack into used red wine barrels for another four months. As an alternative to filling a barrel, you can simply let it sit on the toasted oak (or about 1½ ounces of oak chips); or soak oak chips in your preferred red wine for about a week, then add to the beer in secondary. Sample after a week, then every couple of weeks or so, and rack when the flavor is to your preference.

Let condition for at least six months before serving to allow astringency of elderberries to mellow.

SPICEBUSH

One of our favorite wild plants to use for beer is northern spicebush (*Lindera benzoin*). Spicebush is native to roughly half of the United States, from Texas to Maine and Florida. All of the plant, from leaves to branches and berries is flavorful and historically has been used as teas and as spice additions. Spicebush leaves and branches were used by the Cherokee, Creek, Ojibwa, Rappahannock, and Iroquois to treat a variety of ailments, as well as in tea and—at least for the Cherokee—as a seasoning for opossum and groundhog. Colonial settlers used the berries as a substitute for allspice.

The leaves of the spicebush tree could be described as orange-like, or similar to bitter orange peel, slightly floral, with a touch of woodiness. The branches and twigs are similar, with more aromas of black pepper and camphor. The berries are even more peppery with hints of clove and allspice. A chemical analysis of the leaves shows them to be very high in the compound 6-methyl-5-hepten-2-one, which imparts a sort of pungent green, herbal, and fruity aroma. This compound is used in flavor compositions to help mimic a huge variety of fruits: apple, banana, citrus, date, blackcurrant, mulberry, raspberry, melon, peach, pear, and pineapple. It is also high in beta-caryophyllene, a chemical found in some hops, which can be described as woody. The tree has almost endless applications. It can be used as a substitute for peppercorn or orange peel in saisons or witbier, and both its phenols and fruitiness are an obvious complement for Belgian yeasts. Spicebush's peculiar orange-like woodiness can enhance or take the place of a spectrum of hops that range from citrusy to woody and herbal. In the recipes in this chapter we emphasize the berries alone in the Nettle-Ginger Saison, and the whole plant in the Single Tree: Spicebush. A number of other recipes in this book also make use of spicebush branches and berries. Branches can be substituted with bitter orange peel, while berries can be substituted with peppercorn and allspice (or a combination of the two) if spicebush doesn't grow near you.

HARVESTING

Leaves and Branches

In our experience, spicebush trees are generally found in similar places where you find paw paw: in creek bottoms, rich soil, and on north- and east-facing slopes. It grows vigorously so harvesting from it—including branches and leaves—doesn't seem to hurt the tree. Spicebush branches can be harvested year round, while the leaves are available spring through fall. Leaves, however, can be preserved for use in the winter by drying. The best way to do this is to harvest the whole branch with the leaves attached, and hang the branch upside down from a wire out of direct sunlight until the leaves are dry. You can leave the branch like this or pull the leaves off and stuff them into a container. Make sure the leaves are completely dry before putting them into a container; otherwise they can become moldy.

Berries

Spicebush berries are ripe when they turn bright red and the skin is glossy. They are extremely spicy—try biting just a corner of the berry to see how peppery they are. You can use the berries immediately by pulsing them in a food processor or coffee grinder. You can also preserve them by drying them or roasting them briefly until they turn dark brown to black. They can then be left in a container like a mason jar and used just like black peppercorns.

BREWING

Leaves and Branches

Use the branches conservatively as they can give slightly woody flavors and are more spicy and camphor-like than the leaves. Three 12-inch branches are plenty for a 5-gallon batch. Break them up into pieces a few inches long before putting them into a bag and boiling for 60 minutes.

The leaves can be packed in for an orange-gin-pepper aroma. If adding fresh, break them apart slightly with your hands before putting them into a bag. Try using a quarter pound for a 5-gallon batch, added 10 minutes before the end of the boil. If adding dry, pulse them in a food processor before adding to a bag. Try ¼ pound for a 5-gallon batch.

Berries

The berries are very pungent and a little goes a long way. Pulse 1 to 2 tablespoons of berries in a food processor and add at various points during the boil. You can extract extra bitterness and spice by boiling for longer. A later addition will give a more mild peppery character. We've used them in saisons, tripels, and other Belgian-inspired beers with phenolic yeast strains.

GINGER-SPICEBUSH SAISON

Batch Size: 5 gallons

OG: 1.059

FG: 1.006

ABV: 7.0%

Bitterness: 27 IBU

GRAINS
5 pounds Pilsner
5 pounds Munich
13 ounces crystal 80°L
8 ounces Special B

MASH
Mash in with 4½ gallons water to hit
147 degrees Fahrenheit
Sparge with 7 gallons water at
168 degrees Fahrenheit

HOPS
½ ounce Chinook at 60 minutes

ADDITIONAL INGREDIENTS
2 tablespoons crushed spicebush berry
at 30 minutes (can be substituted
with peppercorns or allspice, or a
combination of the two)
¼ pound ginger, chopped in a food
processor, at 60 minutes

LENGTH OF BOIL
90 minutes with 15-minute whirlpool at
flameout

YEAST
Belgian Saison

FERMENTATION
*Start at 68 degrees Fahrenheit and
allow to rise to 85 degrees naturally.*

SINGLE TREE: SPICEBUSH

Batch Size: 5 gallons

OG: 1.050

FG: 1.011

ABV: 5.1%

Bitterness: 23 IBU

GRAINS
7 pounds Pilsner
2 pounds Munich
10 ounces Special B

MASH
Mash in with 4 gallons water to hit
   147 degrees Fahrenheit
Sparge with 7½ gallons water at
   168 degrees Fahrenheit

HOPS
¾ ounce East Kent Goldings at
   60 minutes
¼ ounce East Kent Goldings at
   10 minutes

ADDITIONAL INGREDIENTS
3 (12-inch-long) spicebush branches at
   60 minutes
¼ pound spicebush leaves at 60 minutes
1 tablespoon crushed spicebush berries
   at 60 minutes

LENGTH OF BOIL
90 minutes with 15-minute whirlpool at
   flameout

YEAST
Belgian Abbey Ale

FERMENTATION
*Start at 68 degrees Fahrenheit for first
two days, and allow to rise a couple of
degrees every day to 80 degrees.*

SUMAC

No, not the poisonous kind.

Unless you are from the Middle East or eastern Mediterranean, you probably aren't terribly familiar with edible varieties of sumac. The red, acidic berries of the sumac shrub have been used traditionally in Middle Eastern cuisine, adding a lemony tartness to salads, meat, hummus, rice, and other dishes. Those who hail from areas of the United States where edible varieties of sumac grow abundantly may remember making sumac-ade, a lemonade-like drink made with sumac berries. (Others living close to poison sumac may remember avoiding sumac entirely.) Use of edible sumac berries generally showcases sumac's peculiar lemon-like tartness.

There are four common edible varieties of sumac that have been used extensively by tribes in North America from as early as 1070 CE: staghorn sumac, smooth sumac, dwarf sumac, and fragrant sumac. None of these are poisonous, and all have hairy red berries, which come together in a cluster or cone shape. Sumac, particularly smooth sumac, was a kind of miracle drug for many Native American tribes. In fact, according to botanist James Duke, of 100 medicinal plants screened for antibiotic activity, smooth sumac was the most active. It was used against colds, as a solution to bedwetting, to treat asthma, diarrhea, dysentery, mouth and throat ulcers, burns, and to treat some sexually transmitted diseases. It was also one of the ingredients added to tobacco during peace pipe ceremonies.

Like rhubarb, sumac is a wonderful addition to beer when a little extra tartness or lemony citrus flavor is wanted. It makes a nice lemon bite for saisons and can be used as a complement to citrusy American hop varieties. It gives a refreshing finish to light summer beers, and helps enhance other fruit, or fruit esters from a variety of yeast strains.

HARVESTING

Sumac berries ripen around July and August and often the cones stay red and harvestable through the winter months, even when the leaves and the rest of the plant has died back. They are less tart in the winter, more bitter, but still edible.

Harvest sumac cones whole. You can clip the cone fairly easily from the rest of the stalk. For brewing the only other preparation is to pull the red berries off the main stalk in the middle. You don't need to rake the berries off individually, just pull them on their stems from the base at the center. Be sure that when you harvest the cones, there have been at least two or three days of sun beforehand, as rain washes off the acidic red powder on the outside of the berries.

Any sumac bush you encounter with red berries is edible. Poison sumac

fermenter. Use about 1 pound for a 5-gallon batch as a starting point to see how you like the tartness. Dial up in later batches if you wish. One unexpected combination we loved was sumac and lavender. Between the tartness of the sumac berries and the cherry-like sweetness of the lavender, it tasted like tart cherry pie.

(*Toxicondendron vernix*) has white berries, and usually grows near swamps. Stick with sumac that has red berries and you won't harvest the wrong kind.

BREWING

Boil sumac berries for 15 minutes in a mesh bag and allow to steep for another 15 minutes in the whirlpool before transferring to a

SUMAC SAISON

Batch Size: 5 gallons

OG: 1.048

FG: 1.005

ABV: 5.7%

Bitterness: 22 IBU

GRAINS
6 pounds 3 ounces Pilsner
2 pounds 6 ounces wheat
12 ounces Munich
2 ounces rice hulls

MASH
Mash in with 4 gallons water to hit
   147 degrees Fahrenheit
Sparge with 7½ gallons water at
   168 degrees Fahrenheit

HOPS
¼ ounce Millenum at 60 minutes
¼ ounce Cluster at 20 minutes

ADDITIONAL INGREDIENTS
1 pound sumac cones (weight is before
   removing berries from main stem) at
   5 minutes

LENGTH OF BOIL
90 minutes with 15-minute whirlpool at
   flameout

YEAST
Belgian Saison

FERMENTATION
*Start at 70 degrees Fahrenheit for first
two days, and allow to rise naturally to
85 degrees.*

YELLOW SWEET CLOVER

Yellow sweet clover is a common roadside plant that, just like Japanese honeysuckle, is not native to the United States but can be found almost anywhere in the country. The plant grows like crazy where it takes hold, and in some parts it has become an intractable weed, crowding out native plants. It is also an important spring wildflower for bees—its Latin name *Melilotus* comes from the word "mel" for honey.

Indeed, yellow sweet clover has almost the same attraction to us humans: its honey-sweetness makes it as good for baking as for beer. It has a sweet, dry aroma we associate with hay (in fact it is often used for hay), while the yellow flowers have the most incredible aroma of bread and vanilla. We've used it as a substitute for vanilla extract in ice cream, and you almost can't tell the difference.

Unfortunately, while yellow sweet clover was introduced because of its many benefits, it has a tendency to crowd out native species. Like all plants, whether we call them weeds or not, there are benefits and drawbacks to having them in our environment. We always hesitate to extol the virtues of plants that crowd out natives, and recommend foraging yellow sweet clover in concert with a plan to maintain a healthy, symbiotic community with native plants.

HARVESTING

Yellow sweet clover flowers between May and September, and we recommend gathering it when it is fully in flower to get the benefit of the vanilla-like blossom. Like honeysuckle, wherever you find yellow sweet clover it will be in abundance, so you can harvest a lot at once. You can use it fresh, or as we typically do: dry the flowers and have them on hand year-round for brewing. Even dried, they maintain their sweet aroma and a little goes a long way.

BREWING

We usually dry the plant first to help concentrate the vanilla-like character and then rake off the leaves and flowers. Add about a half cup of the leaves and flowers to the end of the boil or to the fermenter for a 5-gallon batch.

SWEET CLOVER ALE

Batch Size: 5 gallons
OG: 1.058
FG: 1.014
ABV: 5.8%
Bitterness: 25 IBU

GRAINS
8 pounds 12 ounces Maris Otter
1 pounds 4 ounces Munich
10 ounces crystal 60°L

MASH
Mash in with 4⅓ gallons water to hit
    152 degrees Fahrenheit
Sparge with 6⅕ gallons water at
    168 degrees Fahrenheit

HOPS
½ ounce Nugget at 60 minutes
¼ ounce Hallertauer Mittelfrüh at
    flameout

ADDITIONAL INGREDIENTS
½ cup dried yellow sweet clover leaves
    and flowers

LENGTH OF BOIL
60 minutes with 15-minute whirlpool at
    flameout

YEAST
British Ale

FERMENTATION
*Start at 68 degrees Fahrenheit for one
week and allow to rise naturally above
70 degrees.*

*Add ½ cup dried yellow sweet clover
leaves and flowers to the fermenter after
primary. Cover with water in mason
jar and boil for 10 minutes. Dump all
contents in fermenter.*

BASIL

No herb conjures summer more so than basil. On pizza, in sandwiches, in pesto, on salads with tomato and mozzarella, basil tends to convey freshness, with a robust, almost minty green flavor that bursts with hints of lemon. It tastes like sunlight and gardens. It's the go-to herb for the summer bounty.

We were not the first people to think about putting basil in beer and we certainly won't be the last. This must be due in part to basil's kinship with hops. Not only is basil extremely aromatic, it lends both a spicy edge and a sweet finish—hop-like without the extra bitterness. In fact, varieties of basil contain a handful of the same chemical compounds that are present in varieties of hops. In our experience, basil blends beautifully with both citrusy American hops and spicy noble hops, particularly depending on the variety of basil being used.

There are dozens of different varieties of basil, which all have different flavor and aroma profiles. Lemon basil tastes distinctly like lemon or lemon peel, even quite a bit like citronella (making it also quite similar to citra hops). Purple basil tends to be more spicy, or clove-like. Tulsi or holy basil is almost another plant entirely, sweeter and spicier, with profound clove characteristics and a black cherry-like aroma. Classic Genovese basil seems ideal in pale ales and IPAs, complementing any one of a number of hop varieties and combinations, while tulsi basil is better suited for

darker beers and spicier malts, like rye. It's as fun to mix and match varieties of herbs with different varities of malts, hops, and brewing styles as it is to learn about new hops and utilize them in beer. In seemingly no other plant is the overlap with hops more evident than basil.

HARVESTING

More than likely you'll want to harvest from your basil plants all summer long. The quantity that you will need for beer, however, is much like the quantity that you will need for a big batch of pesto: a large portion of the whole plant. The best way to harvest your basil and to keep the plant alive is to clip the plant from the stem where it splits into new shoots. This is not just where two leaves shoot out, but where full branches or small leaves grow directly from the main stem. New shoots will continue to grow and create more leaves that you can harvest later.

The flavor and aroma of basil changes once harvested and dried, but for brewing this can add a different dimension to your beer. Dried basil loses some of the fresh, green, floral quality and instead retains the spiciness and light mint flavors. You can dry basil and still use it two years later (or more) by pulling the basil out of the ground by its roots, tying the ends of the plants together with twine, and hanging it upside down on a wire or string. Once dry you can leave the plants as they are or remove the leaves and store them in a mason jar.

BREWING

Brewing with basil is much like brewing with hops. You are the captain of your own ship; you can decide how much is too much or not enough. We can say without exception that every single person has a different palate when it comes to basil, much like hops. Some say they can't drink the beer because there's too much basil while others—drinking the same beer—can hardly taste it at all.

To find your ideal threshold, start with six 12-inch plants of fresh basil for a 5-gallon batch. Use the whole plant, including the stem. Although we don't include it in the recipe to follow, we have made several versions of our basil ale with lemon peel (added at flameout), which enhances the aromas of both the hops and the basil. As with juniper, we often add the basil at all points throughout the brewing process: in the hot liquor tank, in the mash tun, as a first wort addition, and at 60 minutes, 30 minutes, and flameout. This helps to infuse the flavor and brings out different flavors and aromas throughout the process. For dried basil, use about ½ cup for a 5-gallon batch, although different varieties of basil have different thresholds of flavor (as you'll see in the difference between Genovese basil and licorice basil). Also, pre-packaged dried basil will be very different from what you dry yourself; we find it sharper and a little bitterer. You'll have to experiment to find out what quantity you prefer.

BASIL ALE

Batch Size: 5 gallons

OG: 1.053

FG: 1.010

ABV: 5.7%

Bitterness: 25 IBU

GRAINS

8 pounds Maris Otter
1 pound rye
1 pound flaked wheat
6 ounces crystal 60°L

MASH

Mash in with 4 gallons water to hit
150 degrees Fahrenheit
Sparge with 6½ gallons water at
168 degrees Fahrenheit

HOPS

½ ounce Nugget at 60 minutes
1 ounce East Kent Goldings at
10 minutes
1 ounce East Kent Goldings at flameout

ADDITIONAL INGREDIENTS

1 (12-inch) fresh Genovese basil plant at
60 minutes
1 (12-inch) fresh Genovese basil plant at
30 minutes
1 (12-inch) fresh Genovese basil plant at
10 minutes
1 (12-inch) fresh Genovese basil plants at
flameout

or

¼ cup dried basil at 30 minutes
¼ cup dried basil at flameout/whirlpool

LENGTH OF BOIL

60 minutes with 15-minute whirlpool at
flameout

YEAST

American Ale

FERMENTATION

*Start at 67 degrees Fahrenheit until
fermentation is almost complete, then
raise to 70 degrees until complete.*

LICORICE BASIL SCHWARZBIER

Batch Size: 5 gallons

OG: 1.049

FG: 1.014

ABV: 4.6%

Bitterness: 25 IBU

GRAINS

6 pounds 8 ounces Pilsner

2 pounds Munich

8 ounces black malt

4 ounces chocolate malt

MASH

Mash in with 4 gallons water to hit
155 degrees Fahrenheit

Sparge with 7½ gallons water at
168 degrees Fahrenheit

HOPS

½ ounce Millennium at 60 minutes

⅓ ounce Saaz at 5 minutes

ADDITIONAL INGREDIENTS

2 tablespoons dried licorice basil, at
flameout (this is for a very subtle
licorice basil flavor; you can another
tablespoon or two without negative
effect). Also try Thai basil and tulsi
basil for different takes on this idea.

LENGTH OF BOIL

90 minutes with 15-minute whirlpool at
flameout

YEAST

American Ale

FERMENTATION

*Start at 62 degrees Fahrenheit for one
week and allow to rise naturally above
70 degrees until fermentation is complete. Alternatively use a lager yeast to
its particular specifications.*

CARROT

Carrots are an ancient cultivated plant found in writings before the Christian Era. Their dual flavors—fresh and spicy when raw, and sweet and caramelly when roasted—and their wealth of vitamins have made them a longtime favorite.

The cultivated carrot we know and love is actually a domesticated version of the wild carrot, often called Queen Anne's Lace. Queen Anne's Lace is distinctive because of its lacy flower heads, but is curiously less often associated with carrot flavor and aroma. In the past, however, seeds were used to infuse carrot-like flavor in food and drink, including beer. And its greens and taproot have the familiar carrot flavor we know from cultivated varieties, albeit slightly spicier, earthier, and a little more bitter. The seeds have an aroma often identified as apricot-like. (The seeds have also been used as a folk contraceptive, although research on this topic is not conclusive.)

Carrots are a great year-round crop that can be harvested at different times, and they store well too. Queen Anne's Lace grows in abundance on our property and we've used the seeds, greens, and roots during different seasons. Wild carrot is a member of the Apiaceae or Umbelliferae family—the parsleys. Other members of the family look very similar and can be highly toxic, like Poison Hemlock. It is critical to know the difference when harvesting, and this is one plant you should be absolutely certain about

when foraging. For those who are hesitant about foraging for wild carrot, but want to try a carrot seed beer, you can harvest the seeds from a known cultivated variety as a substitute (if you're not growing them yourself, ask a farmer to allow some carrots to go to seed).

Also closely related to carrots are parsnips. The two are so similar that they were once considered nearly identical plants. The original wild carrot was a much lighter color, almost white, with a similar distinctive spiciness—hence the association. Today's cultivated parsnips have a fantastic spicy character that often verges on mint and vanillin. We've put it into a lightly smoky black ale and recommend using it in any of the ways we use the carrot tap root in this chapter.

HARVESTING

Taproot and Greens

Carrots are available year round due to successive plantings and cuttings, and are one of the few plants we can harvest in the late winter. Often, fresh young carrots have a sweeter, spicier flavor than older carrots, but both can be just fine for brewing in their own unique ways. Carrots are also a great plant to store. Pack in sand or in the ground at cellar temperature and they will keep up to six months. The greens can be harvested along with the root and add extra carrot flavor.

Seeds

Depending on when a cultivated carrot has been planted, the seeds can be ready to harvest after the greens have produced their umbrella-shaped flowers and the flowers have turned to seed. Wild carrot seed is often harvested in July or August. At that stage, the umbrella-shaped flower head has browned slightly and curled up on itself like a closed fist. We often use the whole seed head, stems and all, since it has the same flavor and aroma as the seeds and requires a lot less work than picking out just the seeds. We have frozen the seed heads for about six months to preserve them, and that seems to work well without losing too much flavor and aroma to freezer burn.

BREWING

Taproot and Greens

We don't use the carrots fresh, but our friend Todd Boera, brewmaster at Fonta Flora Brewery in North Carolina, has experimented extensively using them raw for his carrot IPA, which he's dubbed Alpha vs. Beta Carotene. He uses around 10 pounds of carrot per barrel, or about 1½ pounds for a 5-gallon batch. He says it doesn't matter what color they are, but younger carrots seem to have better flavor.

Todd has experimented with adding the carrots at different stages in the process. He has processed them using a food processor and added them to the fermenter in a strainer bag, and has experimented with juicing all of the carrots and adding the juice directly into the tank. He has shredded the carrots and has added both the shredded carrots and the juice at the very end of fermentation, as well as towards the end of conditioning after dropping the yeast. After all of that experimentation, he says he tends to like the profile of adding juice directly to the conditioning beer. "This allows for the carrot sugars to remain present and not fermented out by the yeast," he says, "It lends a little more body and a nice residual carrot sweetness."

At Scratch we usually roast the carrot roots first to caramelize their natural sugars. We roughly chop the carrot and braise it in our oven with a little water so it doesn't burn, usually around 450 degrees Fahrenheit until it starts to get sweet and browned. Then we add it to the fermenter.

Often we use the greens for bittering. They have a lovely mild carrot aroma and a small amount of bittering character. For a moderate amount of flavor, use just 2 ounces in a 5-gallon batch. You can also use them in combination with other herbs and spices, like peppercorns, ginger, or garden herbs. They should be used fresh.

Seeds

The carrot seeds add a whole other dimension to a beer. Our carrot seed ale utilizes just the seed heads and gives a hint of carrot and a layer of apricot. Use the whole seed head for ease of harvest, only 5 ounces per 5-gallon batch. We've used the seeds both in the boil, for 60 minutes and steeped in the fermenter, as it was traditionally done. Both yield interesting results and are recommended.

CARROT-GINGER SAISON

Batch Size: 5 gallons

OG: 1.054

FG: 1.011

ABV: 5.6%

Bitterness: 33 IBU

GRAINS

8 pounds Pilsner
2 pounds Munich
4 ounces Special B

MASH

Mash in with 4 gallons water to hit
147 degrees Fahrenheit
Sparge with 7½ gallons water at
168 degrees Fahrenheit

HOPS

½ ounce Nugget at 60 minutes
⅔ ounce East Kent Goldings at
15 minutes

ADDITIONAL INGREDIENTS

½ pound fresh ginger, roughly chopped
in a food processor, at 60 minutes
1 tablespoon ground spicebush berries
(you can substitute with black pepper
and/or allspice) at 10 minutes
2 pounds roasted carrots, added into
the fermenter

LENGTH OF BOIL

90 minutes with 15-minute whirlpool at
flameout

YEAST

Belgian Saison

FERMENTATION

*Start at 68 degrees Fahrenheit and
allow to rise naturally to 85 degrees and
above until fermentation is complete.*

*Add the roasted carrots and condition
for another two weeks.*

CARROT SEED ALE

Batch Size: 5 gallons

OG: 1.052

FG: 1.011

ABV: 5.4%

Bitterness: 23 IBU

GRAINS
8 pounds Vienna
2 pounds Munich

MASH
Mash in with 4 gallons water to hit
147 degrees Fahrenheit
Sparge with 6½ gallons water at
168 degrees Fahrenheit

HOPS
½ ounce Nugget at 60 minutes

or

1 pound carrot taproot for bittering at
60 minutes, in place of hops

ADDITIONAL INGREDIENTS
5 ounces carrot seed heads at
60 minutes

LENGTH OF BOIL
60 minutes with 15-minute whirlpool at
flameout

YEAST
American Ale

FERMENTATION
*Ferment at 68 degrees Fahrenheit for
one week and allow to rise to 70 degrees
until fermentation is complete.*

TOMATO

One of the first things Aaron planted at the brewery was tomatoes. The year before we opened our doors, we experimented with about thirty varieties of heirloom tomatoes, largely knowing that we would eventually be using them on pizzas. We wanted to compare their flavor and see how they would grow in our weather. As an experiment, we planted them through the center of our hop rows to gauge space in our garden.

By late summer we were swimming in tomatoes. The garden was a veritable jungle, and it was nearly impossible to harvest tomatoes where the vines had started growing together. The tomatoes between the hop rows did even better. There were Cherokee Purples, Wapsipinicon Peach, Yellow Pear, and Matt's Wild Cherry tomatoes growing in and around the hops. We no longer plant tomatoes between the hops, but we still get volunteers there every year. Particularly hardy have been the Matt's Wild Cherry tomatoes. It is not an uncommon sight to see a hop bine and a tomato vine circling around one another on the hop trellis.

Tomatoes, like apples, have suffered from years of industrial farming that emphasizes color and shelf life over flavor and seasonality. They are also a plant that gives untold rewards when you plant at home and harvest in-season, or when you buy heirloom varieties directly from a farmer. There is nothing as fresh, vibrant, juicy, and flavorful than a tomato just harvested from the vine.

Unfortunately, tomatoes in commercial beer in the United States have been used in ways that mimic cocktails like Bloody Marys and in combinations like tomato and clam juice. The reason for this may be that beer has been blended into cocktails with tomatoes for a long time, but tomatoes themselves haven't been considered a fermentable ingredient. Interestingly, one of the more inspiring places to see the tomato's potential in drink is wine. Anyone who hasn't had tomato wine may be surprised to know that once the juice has been fermented to alcohol, the result is not like tomato sauce. Depending on the tomatoes used, the wine can taste dry and tropical. Omerto, a winery in Quebec, Canada, claims to be the world's first commercial tomato wine venture, making wines that range in flavor from something akin to a (slightly more alcoholic) Sauvignon Blanc to a white Port. Omerto uses a blend of heirloom tomatoes, as the flavor is more pronounced and dynamic. Taking a wine-maker's tack on using tomatoes is the best way we can think of to utilize tomatoes in beer, particularly the emphasis on full-flavored heirloom varieties.

We have used tomatoes fresh and dried, and there are dozens of different angles you can take with the fruit that we can suggest as a result of what we've learned from our experiments. Tomatoes are an unusual plant to use for beer, but one with promising results we hope to learn more about after even more experimentation.

HARVESTING

Tomatoes are a classic mid-summer fruit, best when eaten the same day they are picked. However, tomatoes will also last for several days on the counter (not in the fridge).

Tomatoes can also be picked green and eaten in that early state of development. We pickle our year-end green tomatoes and serve them at the brewery as an appetizer. You can also keep green tomatoes and allow them to ripen off the vine—this is great for a batch of year-end tomatoes picked before the first frost. Place them in a closed paper bag in a relatively cool place. Try not to put too much pressure on the tomatoes. Stack in only one or two layers, with the biggest tomatoes on the bottom. Over time, if there is too much pressure on the tomatoes, they will bruise and then rot in the bag.

Finally, tomatoes can also be preserved from a ripened state by dehydration. We've had great success drying cherry tomatoes whole, and in slicing up bigger tomatoes and drying the slices. We use a standard dehydrator and save the tomatoes in Mason jars. They're good for several years after fully drying.

BREWING

Below are five different ways we suggest brewing with tomatoes. Some are based on our experience at the brewery and others are suggestions from our understanding of the plant, experimentation, and uses in wine.

Fresh

Fresh tomatoes give a surprisingly mild flavor to beer and tend to ferment fully, like any other fruit. Use about two gallons of fresh tomatoes per gallon of beer. Chop or puree them (leaving the skins on is fine). If you're worried about infection, you can add them to the end of the boil; otherwise they can go into the fermenter after primary fermentation is complete.

Dried

Our Belgian Dark Strong recipe included here was our favorite tomato beer. The dried cherry tomatoes retain a ton of their perceived sweetness and became raisiny and prune-like, the same way that grapes do when dried. They blend perfectly with a Belgian yeast strain. Every tomato will be a little different when dried, depending on what it was like when ripe. In general, though, dried tomatoes keep a lot of the tomato character we associate with the fruit, and so are better in slightly maltier beers, particularly with English or Belgian yeasts that emphasize stone fruit esters.

Green

Green tomatoes have a crisp acidity that mellows out as the fruit ripens. We've never brewed with them, but Marika uses them a lot in cooking at the end of the season, and has been itching to do a green tomato beer for some time. (Unfortunately, they usually end up in curry, a similar ending to the story of our best of intentions to brew with morel mushrooms.) We would recommend emphasizing the tartness of the tomato by brewing a lighter saison-style beer with a relatively dry finish, at a rate of about 2 pounds of tomatoes per gallon. This should give a significantly tart flavor and finish.

Brett and Bacteria

Speaking of tart and dry, tomatoes make a natural complement to wild yeast strains. In addition to a normal *Saccharomyces* fermentation, tomatoes can be enhanced by strains of *Brettanomyces* or even *Lactobacillus* or other tart bacteria. Again, we think of this a bit like wine, where the aim would be to create a beer that's dry, fruity, perhaps a little tropical, with a nice cleansing acidity.

Kettle souring with *Lactobacillus* is a good technique to control tartness for anyone just dabbling in sour beer. Fermenting with a *Brettanomyces* strain that emphasizes tropical notes would be good for tomatoes that would also naturally give citrus flavors in the fermentation.

Barrel-aging

Next logical step? Put that brew in a barrel! Any of these techniques can be enhanced with some oak, or even finished with a wild culture on oak. There seems to be a natural connection between tomatoes and grapes— any Italian knows this instinctively—so any wine-making technique you use should give interesting results in tomato beer.

SUN-DRIED CHERRY TOMATO DARK STRONG

Batch Size: 5 gallons

OG: 1.083

FG: 1.014

ABV: 9.2%

Bitterness: 33 IBU

GRAINS

11 pounds 12 ounces Pilsner

1 pound 12 ounces Munich

1 pound 4 ounces Special B

14 ounces flaked wheat

7 ounces aromatic malt

MASH

Mash in with 6 gallons water to hit
150 degrees Fahrenheit

Sparge with 6 gallons water at
168 degrees Fahrenheit

HOPS

2 ounces Willamette at 60 minutes

ADDITIONAL INGREDIENTS

1 ounce golden raisins at flameout

1 pint jar worth of sun-dried cherry
tomatoes at flameout

LENGTH OF BOIL

90 minutes with 15-minute whirlpool at
flameout

YEAST

Belgian Abbey Ale

FERMENTATION

*Ferment at 68 degrees Fahrenheit for
one week and allow to rise to 80 degrees
until fermentation is complete.*

GREEN TOMATO SAISON

Batch Size: 5 gallons
OG: 1.052
FG: 1.005
ABV: 6.2%
Bitterness: 25 IBU

GRAINS
10 pounds Pilsner

MASH
Mash in with 4 gallons water to hit 147 degrees Fahrenheit
Sparge with 7½ gallons water at 168 degrees Fahrenheit

HOPS
⅓ ounce Nugget at 60 minutes
1 ounce Citra at flameout

ADDITIONAL INGREDIENTS
10 pounds green tomatoes, puréed in food processor and added to boil at flameout in very fine mesh bag (add juice that may come through the bag as you're adding tomatoes to the boil as well)

LENGTH OF BOIL
90 minutes with 15-minute whirlpool at flameout

YEAST
Belgian Saison

FERMENTATION
Begin fermentation at 70 degrees Fahrenheit and allow to rise naturally to 85 degrees or above until fermentation is complete.

Add more Citra (or any other citrusy or tropical hop) to the fermenter after primary fermentation is complete to enhance aroma, if desired

FENNEL

Fennel has a long history in food and drink. It was a common herbal component for meads in the Middle Ages, is a key ingredient in licorice, and it is one of the main botanicals in absinthe. It has a voluminous culinary history in Asia, the Middle East, and the Mediterranean (where it is native), and promises an equally bountiful harvest where it grows. The word "marathon," famous now for the race that ended in the city called Marathon in Greece, is in fact a term that refers to the famous site being overgrown with fennel.

Fennel is by no means delicate. It is a distinctive, pungent, love-it-or-hate-it plant that many people (at least in the United States) associate with breath fresheners or candy. That said, it can be used with more subtlety than is found in a typical stick of black licorice. Fennel flowers have a unique floral character, while the bulb is milder with a celery undertone. The seeds are well known to anyone who makes sausage or who may have picked up a candy-coated after-dinner treat in an Indian restaurant; they contain some of the most pungent expressions of anethole, the anise-like compound that gives it its distinct flavor. A little bit of any part of fennel goes a long way.

The entire plant can be used in brewing: bulb, stalk, leaves, flower, and seeds. If you buy fennel and only need to use the bulb for a dish you're cooking for dinner, keep the stalks and leaves to put into a beer. There will be more than enough for what you need in a 5-gallon batch, and it can make for a refreshing, mint or licorice-like finish to any beer.

HARVESTING

Bulb, Stalk, and Leaves

Grown as a garden herb, fennel fronds are cut regularly for salads and for use with fish, and can be used from summer through fall if cut back routinely this way.

If you keep the plant trimmed throughout the year, the whole plant from the bulb up can be harvested before the first frost, or at any point after the plant is large enough to flower. Most often the plant you find at the grocery store or the farmers' market will be in this state, either just the bulb or the bulb and the stalks.

If your garden-grown plant does happen to get away from you, though, and it flowers or starts to go to seed early, have no fear. As with so many other plants, it doesn't matter what fennel looks like for brewing, and very often the flavor is just as good, or even slightly more pronounced. Don't waste it! If a friend or farmer is letting their plant go to seed and can't use all their stalks and bulbs, volunteer to use this slightly less pretty plant for beer.

Flowers and Seeds

If the plant *does* go to seed, consider simply harvesting the seeds. Both the flowers and seeds are as good for beer as the rest of the plant. Simply allow the plant to develop its small yellow flowers, and then cut the heads as they open up; or let them continue to develop seeds. Seeds can be collected and stored for use at any time throughout the year.

BREWING

Bulb, Stalk, and Leaves

When used in mild doses, fennel does more than just taste like licorice. It has a smooth sweetness that can complement a variety of estery ale yeasts. We found that it blends beautifully with Belgian stone fruit esters and can also round out the chocolate and coffee notes of satiny stouts. You can get this subtle finish using just a small amount of the bulb, stalk, and/or leaves. Just 3 ounces in a 5-gallon batch in the fermenter will do the trick; or, use one bulb split up throughout the boil, with leaves and stalks added toward flameout.

Flowers and Seeds

Flowers have a powerful aroma and only a few are needed to add flavor to beer. One flower head in a 5-gallon batch will add a moderately strong floral anise character. Add to the fermenter to control the degree of flavor. Check after just one day and continue checking until the beer is to your liking.

Seeds should be roughly broken up with a mortar and pestle or in a coffee grinder. A tablespoon should lend a distinctively licorice-like aroma to any beer. Consider blending them with several other seeds, herbs, and roots to create an herbal concoction similar to absinthe.

BELGIAN FENNEL STOUT

Batch Size: 5 gallons

OG: 1.063

FG: 1.012

ABV: 6.7%

Bitterness: 27 IBU

GRAINS
5 pounds 8 ounces Vienna
4 pounds 8 ounces Munich
1 pound chocolate malt
12 ounces crystal 80°L
4 ounces Special B
4 ounces roasted barley

MASH
Mash in with 5 gallons water to hit
    152 degrees Fahrenheit
Sparge with 6 gallons water at
    168 degrees Fahrenheit

HOPS
⅔ ounce Nugget at 60 minutes
⅔ ounce East Kent Goldings at
    5 minutes

ADDITIONAL INGREDIENTS
½ fennel bulb at 60 minutes
½ fennel bulb, split between the
    40-minute, 20-minute, and flameout
    marks
2½ ounce leaves and flowers at flameout
1 flower head into fermenter, if desired

LENGTH OF BOIL
60 minutes with 15-minute whirlpool at
    flameout

YEAST
Belgian Abbey Ale

FERMENTATION
Begin fermentation at 66 degrees Fahrenheit for two days, and allow to rise a couple of degrees every day until it hits 75 degrees.

Add the head of the fennel to the fermenter if you want more flavor.

THE HERBS OF ABSINTHE

Absinthe's distinctive flavor is due in large part to a trio of herbs: grande wormwood, anise, and fennel. Numerous other plants have been combined as supporting players, such as hyssop, mint, calamus root, chamomile, angelica, coriander, and star anise. However, wormwood is the star of the show. The Latin name for grande wormwood, the type used in absinthe, is *Artemisia absinthium*, a title irrevocably linked with the name of the drink. However, wormwood infusions, whether in water, beer, spirits, or wine, have been used since ancient times for their purported health benefits. It wasn't until about 1792 that Pierre Ordinaire, a French doctor living in Switzerland, concocted an herbal infusion of wormwood, anise, and other herbs. This drink would circle through Paris and the many artists and illuminati living there in the nineteenth century before gaining worldwide fame. It was during those heady times that the absinthe we recognize today was born.

And then it was banned.

Wormwood contains thujone, which was thought to induce hallucinations and is part of the reason absinthe was effectively banned in the United States. Science, however, helped to clear wormwood's name. Thujone content in wormwood was measured through the use of gas chromatography mass spectrometry, and was found in many cases to be under the U.S. government limit of 10 parts per million (ppm), making it (in a regulatory sense) thujone-free. This is what allowed absinthe—even varieties that were made using traditional recipes—to be sold again in the United States starting in 2007. Wormwood is available through many homebrew stores and can be used to infuse bitterness in beer, just as it has been used in spirits for centuries. It can be mixed and matched with fennel, anise, and a variety of herbs in this book to create something as beguiling as one of the world's most intoxicating (literally and figuratively!) spirits.

LAVENDER

Several months after we opened, Marika surprised some Italian friends with a visit to Abruzzo on the occasion of their wedding. It was July in the Appenines, up in the mountains a few hours east of Rome, and everything was green. The sisters of the bride wanted to create something to commemorate the day, so they hunted for a plant that we could put into a beer that would remind the newlyweds of July in Abruzzo—to be opened a year later on their anniversary. It wasn't hard to find just the thing: lavender was blooming everywhere. It was impossible to escape its intoxicating fragrance, as bushes literally surrounded the roads and buildings of the little *agriturismo* in Forca di Penne.

So we had lavender—great, but how to incorporate it into a beer? Lavender is a tricky plant. Most often used in soaps and lotions, it's hard not to be reminded of skin care products when smelling it. Wonderfully aromatic, yes, but perhaps not ideal for beer.

However, there is something bewitching about the velvety texture of lavender and its corresponding aroma which pushed us to experiment with it, and even to cultivate some extra plants in our herb garden in southern Illinois. After some tinkering, we have found that the best way to incorporate lavender isn't by using the flowers at all, but by using the leaves and stems of the plant, or by drying the flowers first to moderate their floral quality. Counterintuitively, boiling the plant for some time, as opposed to putting it

directly into the fermenter, reduces the flowery aroma as well. These techniques emphasize other elements that are often lost to the floral nature we associate with soaps, instead allowing the other cinnamon and cherry-like flavors in this luxurious plant to shine.

HARVESTING

Leaves and Stems

As soon as the plant has grown and is about to flower, its leaves will be just right to use in beer, and they will continue to be available throughout the summer and fall. Best of all, because lavender is such an aromatic plant, it works well when dried for use in brewing throughout the winter as well. When using fresh lavender, harvest the portions of the stems (with leaves attached) above the ground and use directly as-is in a hop bag in the boil.

To preserve for later use, harvest the whole plant out of the ground before the first frost and dry in a dehydrator or by tying a string around the bottom of the stems and hanging on a wall or over a wire. Once dry, you can pull the leaves off and put them in a mason jar, or just simply leave the plant tied together and put it directly into beer whole.

Flowers

Depending on your climate, lavender will most likely flower in June or July. Cut the blooms off the top of the plant and allow them to dry in a dehydrator or simply by setting out on a screen or a bowl through which air can move. These will stay good for brewing for a couple of years without losing much of their aromatic quality.

BREWING

Leaves and Stems

You will be amazed at the flavor and aroma you will get after boiling lavender for 60 minutes. We have come to prefer this method, as it brings the cinnamon and cherry flavors, rather than the soapy floral aroma we usually associate with the plant, to the forefront. We have found that these flavors can be wonderful in a wide variety of styles of beer, and they go particularly well with the cherry esters of the Belgian yeast strain in our Lavender Tripel. A little goes a long way. Try two 6-inch sprigs at 60 minutes before the end of the boil.

Flowers

The first beer we created with lavender was Il Fortino, named after Marika's friends' *agriturismo* in Italy. We attempted to make a beer with a velvety mouthfeel and a rich, creamy body to mimic the texture of the lavender. An oatmeal stout seemed ideal. The leaves and stems weren't quite aromatic enough, so we added some dried flowers to the fermenter and after only 24 hours it was ready to keg—a testament to how powerful the flowers can be. It also goes to show that you can adjust your flavor and aroma additions if they're not perfect to start, and in this case the dried flowers added just enough to be evident but not overpowering. To boost the lavender aroma of your beer try adding just 2 tablespoons of dried flowers in the fermenter, and sample after 24 hours.

IL FORTINO

Batch Size: 5 gallons

OG: 1.074

FG: 1.016

ABV: 7.7%

Bitterness: 43 IBU

GRAINS
10 pounds 12 ounces Maris Otter
1 pound 8 ounces flaked oats
12 ounces black malt
10 ounces chocolate malt
4 ounces Special B
4 ounces roasted barley

MASH
Mash in with 5½ gallons water to hit
150 degrees Fahrenheit
Sparge with 5½ gallons water at
168 degrees Fahrenheit

HOPS
1 ounce Chinook at 60 minutes
1 ounce East Kent Goldings at
20 minutes

ADDITIONAL INGREDIENTS
2 (6-inch-long) sprigs fresh lavender
(stems and leaves both) at flameout
2 tablespoons dried lavender flowers to
fermenter

LENGTH OF BOIL
60 minutes with 15-minute whirlpool at
flameout

YEAST
British Ale

FERMENTATION
Begin fermentation at 66 degrees Fahrenheit for two days and allow to rise a couple of degrees every day until it hits 75 degrees.

Add the dried lavender flowers and sample after 24 hours. Taste and rack to your liking.

LAVENDER TRIPEL

Batch Size: 5 gallons

OG: 1.076

FG: 1.006

ABV: 9.3%

Bitterness: 24 IBU

GRAINS
10 pounds Pilsner
2 pounds cane sugar
1 pound flaked oats

MASH
Mash in with 5½ gallons water to hit
150 degrees Fahrenheit
Sparge with 5½ gallons water at
168 degrees Fahrenheit

HOPS
¾ ounce Citra at 60 minutes
1 ounce East Kent Goldings at
20 minutes

ADDITIONAL INGREDIENTS
3 (6-inch-long) sprigs lavender (stems
and leaves) at 60 minutes
1 (6-inch-long) sprig of lavender (stems
and leaves) at flameout

LENGTH OF BOIL
90 minutes with 15-minute whirlpool at
flameout

YEAST
Belgian Abbey Ale

FERMENTATION
Begin fermentation at 68 degrees Fahrenheit for two days and allow to rise a couple of degrees every day until it hits 80 degrees.

PEACH

We are lucky to live in a vital peach-growing region in southern Illinois, aided by our moderately cold winters and warm summers. At the height of July and August, the Shawnee hills are polka-dotted pink and red for miles along some of the most scenic hillsides from Murphysboro to Cobden, and among the many Amish communities in between.

Peaches have an ancient history: originating in China, traveling to continental Europe through Persia, and then crossing to the United States early during its colonization. They were introduced to the St. Simons and Cumberland Islands along Georgia's coast by Franciscan monks as early as 1571, and were cultivated by the Cherokee by the 1700s. Peaches and nectarines are genetically nearly identical, with the main difference being the peach's fuzzy exterior. The two can be used more or less interchangeably.

Peaches are an ideal addition to beer. Their bright acidity assures that some of their flavor will come through even after most of their sweet sugars have fermented away. Peach aroma in particular is retained after fermentation, making it a great accompaniment to Belgian yeasts or other strains that create stone fruit esters.

HARVESTING

Most of us know a ripe peach when we see, feel, and smell one: slightly soft and aromatic, often—though not always—bright red. The simplest peaches for beer-making are freestone peaches, as it is easier to remove the pit when preparing them to add to the beer. That said, some heirloom varieties are clingstones, so they're harder to process—but can add a lot of extra flavor.

Ripe peaches should be used almost immediately. After their peak, they will quickly lose flavor and aroma and start to pick up nail polish-like off flavors. Peaches don't take well to freezing; however, they can be canned if it's necessary to preserve them to add later. The canning process, however, will unfortunately cook out some of the brightness of the fruit when fresh. There is no comparison (in both flavor and aroma) to using a fresh, juicy peach just days off the tree.

BREWING

Peaches can be added both to the end of the boil and to the fermenter, but both methods deliver slightly different results. Because of their furry exterior, yeasts and other bacteria have the tendency to cling to peach skins. We have had an instance of *Acetobacter* infection when adding peaches directly to the fermenter, since it is hard to remove the bacteria entirely when using fresh fruit. Of course, you can remove the skins of the peaches. However, this requires touching the fruit more with your hands, a very clean cutting board and knife, and a sanitized container which can keep out bugs while you're working.

The best method we have found to preserve the peach's unique aroma is to put whole peaches into a bucket of sanitizing solution for at least 5 minutes, and then take each fruit out one by one, cut it into quarters or sixths, place it (skin-on) into a sterilized nylon bag which has been boiled for 15 minutes, and then add to the fermenter for roughly four to five days. The nylon bag keeps the peaches from clogging the racking arm in our fermenters, but with a normal 5-gallon carboy or bucket, you should be able to add the peaches directly to the fermenter and rack above them.

Most of the beers we've brewed with peaches have been blonde to amber Belgian styles. (They are wonderful with a spicy wit yeast and a little coriander.) If your beer is darker or maltier and your aim is not about extracting the brightness or acidity from the peach so much as the darker stone-fruit flavors, then adding the peaches to the end of the boil is a better alternative. This almost guarantees that you will kill any yeast or bacteria on the skins of the fruit. Simply cut the peaches into quarters or sixths and put the pieces into a nylon bag at the end of the boil. Roughly chopping in a food processor will also help give more surface-area contact and a little more flavor and aroma. We recommend at least 8 pounds of peaches for a 5-gallon batch, no matter what method you use to add the peach to the beer.

An alternative is to add the peaches to the end of the boil so that they are bathed in sterilizing wort while the juice is extracted. This method nearly eliminates the chance of infection, but it also cooks the peaches and you lose some of the bright flavor and aroma—just as you would if you were using canned peaches. You can use nectarines as an alternative since their slick skin makes it harder for bacteria to cling and hide.

PEACH OAK ABBEY

Batch Size: 5 gallons

OG: 1.064

FG: 1.007

ABV: 7.4%

Bitterness: 22 IBU

GRAINS
5 pounds Vienna
5 pounds Munich
1 pound cane sugar
7 ounces Special B

MASH
Mash in with 4½ gallons water to hit
  150 degrees Fahrenheit
Sparge with 7 gallons water at
  168 degrees Fahrenheit

HOPS
½ ounce Nugget at 60 minutes

ADDITIONAL INGREDIENTS
8 pounds peaches, chopped in a food
  processor, added to the last 5 minutes
  of the boil in a mesh bag

LENGTH OF BOIL
90 minutes with 15-minute whirlpool at
  flameout

YEAST
Belgian Abbey Ale

FERMENTATION
*Begin fermentation at 68 degrees Fahr-
enheit for two days and allow to rise a
couple of degrees every day until it hits
80 degrees.*

*Soak 1 medium toast American oak
spiral in your favorite whiskey for
3 days, then add spiral to the fermenter
after primary fermentation is complete.
Rack to taste.*

*Alternatively, toast one 16-inch x 3-inch
chunk of fresh oak heartwood and add to
fermenter after primary fermentation.
Check after one week and rack to taste.*

GOOSEBERRY

Gooseberries and currants are cousins in the *Ribes* genus. They are both tart berries with a slight astringency that makes them often difficult to consume raw, but wonderful for jams, pies, and puddings.

Gooseberries taste like lemon and kiwi and are exceptionally tart when green, becoming sweeter and less bright and acidic as they age and turn purple. Perhaps due to their natural acidity, they have been used for centuries to make wine. One of the earliest mentions is in Martha Washington's famous cookbook, a collection with recipes dating back to the Jacobean and Elizabethan era. Gooseberries are naturally high in pectin, and this may be one reason the recipe also suggests running the liquid through a jelly bag at one point. (We've never had to do this with beer, although the beer will remain cloudy.)

You can use gooseberries at any stage in their development, depending on your preference. They have traditionally been used in pies and preserves when green because their acidity makes an enticing blend with sugar, the way tart cherries or cranberries would. Their tartness also makes them an excellent foil for the residual sugars in beer, and they complement all varieties of dry or lightly tart ales like saisons, witbiers, or Berliner weisse; they would also make a great alternative to raspberry or cherry in lambic. Even Martha Washington would

have known this. Her recipe says that the process for making gooseberry wine would be just as good for raspberries, mulberries, blackberries, or peaches. We have also found that while currants and gooseberries are quite similar, some variation does exist. Black currants tend to be more astringent and phenolic than bright and cheerful gooseberries. But these are just the many happy variations that allow us to play with all of these similar tart fruits—mulberry, gooseberry, and currant alike.

HARVESTING

We use gooseberries green for their tart zestiness and recommend harvesting them at this stage, usually around June in southern Illinois. At this point they are tough and there is little worry of crushing them. If not using immediately, green gooseberries freeze well. Gooseberries have little tops and tails that usually need to be trimmed when using for food, but these can be left on for brewing since their texture isn't important.

Cultivation of gooseberries (and currants) is illegal in certain states because the plant can be a host for white pine blister rust, which can cause severe damage to American white pines. It is therefore not grown everywhere in the United States, and you should check your state regulations before planting yourself.

BREWING

Once picked, we use the gooseberries within two days. We puree them finely in a food processor, then steep them in a mesh bag during the last 5 minutes of the boil. (If using frozen gooseberries, allow them to thaw first.) As mentioned before, the berries are naturally high in pectin, which will cause some haze in your finished beer.

Since gooseberries are not available fresh everywhere, you may look for alternatives at your local grocery store. There are both canned and frozen versions, though they may have to be special ordered (both are available online). We recommend the frozen version for beer. Canned versions are fine for pies since they come in syrup and will be slightly mushy; but for beer, the frozen version will retain more of the acidity without extra sugar from the syrup, and will be easier to add to the boil or fermenter.

GOOSEBERRY GOLDEN

Batch Size: 5 gallons
OG: 1.062
FG: 1.015
ABV: 6.2%
Bitterness: 26 IBU

GRAINS
8 pounds Pilsner
3 pounds Vienna
1 pound crystal 40°L

MASH
Mash in with 4½ gallons water to hit
    150 degrees Fahrenheit
Sparge with 7 gallons water at
    168 degrees Fahrenheit

HOPS
½ ounce Nugget at 60 minutes
1 ounce Styrian Goldings at flameout

ADDITIONAL INGREDIENTS
8 pounds gooseberries, finely chopped
    in a food processor. Place processed
    fruit in a mesh bag and add to the
    boil at 60 minutes.

LENGTH OF BOIL
90 minutes with 15-minute whirlpool at
    flameout

YEAST
Belgian Abbey Ale

FERMENTATION
Begin fermentation at 68 degrees Fahrenheit for two days and allow to rise a couple of degrees every day until it hits 80 degrees.

PAW PAW

The common paw paw produces the largest edible fruit indigenous to North America. It is also the only tropical fruit tree that grows as far north in the Americas. Its interior flesh is the texture of custard and tastes like banana and mango, with huge triangular seeds that were used as jewelry by Native Americans.

Like clockwork, every first week of September the paw paws start dropping in our part of southern Illinois. Unfortunately what is slightly more unpredictable is which trees will produce fruit. Paw paw flowers give off an odor similar to rotting meat, great for attracting pollinators like blow flies and carrion beetles, but lacking a wider appeal—so many (if not most) paw paw trees do not produce fruit. Farmers who cultivate paw paw often hang meat near trees to entice these forest friends to pollinate their trees.

That said, there are some groves, deep in the woods, where one can find paw paws in abundance. Down an old country road so overgrown the gravel only peeks through in patches is southern Illinois forest so lush you'd think you were in Costa Rica. A half-mile walk past the end of the road and you will smell the unmistakable papaya and mango aromas of paw paw. Suddenly, as you scan the forest floor you'll see dozens, even hundreds of potato-sized yellow, green, and brown-spotted fruits scattered in clumps under old looming paw paw trees with huge banana-size leaves.

What you find as you humbly begin to harvest these tropical treasures is that you are already too late—the beetles, ants, and flies, permanent residents of these grounds, have already started excavating the fruit for themselves. For every one fruit you pick up you will probably have to leave five or six to the insects. Wafting alongside the mango aromas is a touch of vinegar as the fruits begin to ferment on the ground.

As much as hunting for mushrooms, hunting for paw paws takes place in secret nooks and sacred grounds. Know the right place and you can carry 50 or 60 pounds of paw paws out of the woods with you after an hour or two. But in most places, usually the most trafficked, the gleaming paw paw trees shine back with nothing but their almost cartoonishly broad leaves.

A warning: the seeds, leaves, and bark of the paw paw contain natural insecticides called acetogenins, which may cause nerve degeneration and possible vision problems. Paw paw is one tree in which the fruit only should be ingested.

HARVESTING

Paw paws grow well in creek bottoms, and on north- and east-facing slopes in moist fertile soil. Pick fruits with the least amount of insect damage. It's still possible to use fruit with one or two small holes or very soft brown spots. Those spots can usually be cut away when you're processing them.

If you come upon unripe fruit, spread it out in a single layer on a baking sheet at room temperature until ripe, usually two to three days. Keep an eye on it, however, since fruit flies are attracted to it.

In general, it is best to process the fruit immediately, since it ripens—and overripens—very quickly. The best method we've found for separating the skins and seeds from the fruit is by mashing the paw paws through some kind of strainer. We typically use a conical stainless mesh strainer with a wooden pestle, or we use the false bottom from our home brew mash tun with a rubber spatula while resting a bowl underneath to catch the pulp. Press the whole fruit through either kind of strainer; the flesh is so soft that the pulp will go through the small holes and the skins and seeds will stay above and can be discarded.

Once you've pulped your paw paw, you can cover it and put it in a refrigerator if you plan on brewing within a week. Or you can put it into 1-gallon freezer bags and keep it in the freezer indefinitely.

BREWING

Paw paws are an obvious choice to use as one would use tropical fruit in beer, as well as to enhance Belgian fruit flavors and aromas or in German styles like Hefeweizen or Weisenbock. Cooking them over high heat will brown them like bananas in brown sugar, giving incredible flavors reminiscent of crème brûlée. Consider using the pulp straight or caramelized for two slightly different takes on the fruit flavor. A quart of pulp in a 5-gallon batch will be enough to allow a subtle (but not overwhelming) amount of flavor to come through in the finished product.

Using Straight Pulp

As you will notice when harvesting these fruits, bugs love them. Pulping them with the skin on, which is nearly the only way to do so, mashes whatever yeast and bacteria that is on the outside of the skin into the pulp. Even if you were to carefully peel the skin, you will inevitably deal with fruit that has been bored into or has one or two bad spots, nearly ensuring a possible infection. Using straight pulp, then, we recommend adding the fruit to the end of the boil, long enough to sterilize it but not so long that it cooks out the flavor and aroma. If frozen, allow it to thaw and add to the last 15 minutes of the boil.

Using Caramelized Pulp

Caramelizing the fruit will cook it at high heat and kill any yeast or bacteria that may have been mashed into the pulp. This allows you to add the paw paw directly to the fermenter. When caramelizing, cook for around 20 minutes on medium heat until the pulp browns—but don't allow it to burn. You can either add it directly to the fermenter or freeze and add it later. If freezing, allow it to warm back up to room temperature (in a sealed container) before adding to the fermenter. The pulp should settle to the bottom and you can rack into kegs or bottles above.

PAW PAW ABBEY

Batch Size: 5 gallons

OG: 1.064

FG: 1.010

ABV: 7.1%

Bitterness: 22 IBU

GRAINS

9 pounds Pilsner

2 pounds flaked wheat

1 pound 8 ounces flaked oats

8 ounces Special B

4 ounces crystal 40°L

MASH

Mash in with 5 gallons water to hit
149 degrees Fahrenheit

Sparge with 7 gallons water at
168 degrees Fahrenheit

HOPS

½ ounce Nugget at 60 minutes

ADDITIONAL INGREDIENTS

1 quart caramelized paw paws added to
the fermenter

LENGTH OF BOIL

90 minutes with 15-minute whirlpool at
flameout

YEAST

Belgian Abbey Ale

FERMENTATION

Begin fermentation at 68 degrees Fahrenheit for two days and allow to rise a couple of degrees every day until it hits 80 degrees.

Add the caramelized pawpaws after primary fermentation is complete. Condition for another one to two weeks.

FALL

Nature slows as the days get shorter and the nights get cooler. Wild greens like dandelion and dock that died off in the heat of the summer may reappear briefly. Note the seed heads on plants of interest—this will prove useful in the winter when only that part of the plant remains. Look for nuts just fallen on the ground and the last of the annual fruits. Dried, dead leaves from oak, maple, and hickory litter the ground and make good bittering additions. Just before the first frost, put the garden to bed, gathering herbs, harvesting and preserving roots, gourds, and the last fruits.

WHAT TO LOOK FOR:

Roots: Dock, Chicory, Rose, Blackberry, Dandelion

Nuts: Acorns, Hickory, Pecans, Black Walnuts

Seeds: Lotus, Sumac, Perilla, Fennel, Garden Herbs

Leaves: Wild Grape, Oak, Maple, Sassafras, Spicebush, Hickory

Wild Fruit: Wild Pear, Paw Paw, Autumn Olive, Perismmon, Wild Grape

Gourds: Pumpkin, Squash

Tubers: Sweet Potatoes, Potatoes

Mushrooms: Turkey Tail

Farm and Market: Apple, Pear, Grape, Arugula, Beets, Radishes, Parsnip, Burdock, Kale, Beet, Green Tomatoes, Salsify, Turnip, Lemongrass, Garden Herbs, Horseradish, Ginger, Turmeric

HICKORY

We are surrounded by hickory trees at the brewery, mostly shagbark and pignut. It is not uncommon in the fall to hear a clang like a gun shot of a hickory nut falling on the roof of the pavilion, or to see shells of nuts inscribed with tiny teeth marks littered over picnic tables where the squirrels have been working to store for the winter.

Hickory is a tree with a deep American heritage and, like oak, is a source of life for human beings. There are about a dozen different hickory trees native to the United States. As a sturdy hard wood, hickory makes fine tools, is good for burning, and is often used to smoke meat. Its nuts were a delicacy for some Native American tribes, and the sap and bark of the shagbark hickory was used as a sugar. The nuts were also used for broth by homesteaders since they have only a mild bitterness. We may not consume as many hickory nuts these days, but everyone is familiar with the pecan, which is a type of hickory. The Chippewa used even green shoots on the trees as a treatment for headaches.

Today we most commonly see hickory used for furniture and BBQ, which is a shame because the whole tree has so much more to offer. Hickory is one of our all-time favorite plants for brewing, as every part has a distinct flavor that can be used in myriad ways, and it has something available to the homebrewer all year round.

HARVESTING

Leaves

We use the leaves green from the tree, dried from the ground, and dried on the branch. Green leaves from the tree have a slightly greener, tannic bitterness; dried leaves from the ground are a little less potent with a similar papery tannic bitterness. If a tree falls or if we've had to remove a tree on our property, we'll break off branches that still have leaves on them and hang them to allow the leaves to dry on the branch. This is just another way to preserve the leaves to brew throughout the winter.

Nuts

We also use hickory nuts and hulls both in their green and brown stages. Hickory and pecan nuts are technically drupes, essentially stone fruit, like peaches, except the fruit is much tougher and the "nut" we eat is the seed. When they initially fall from the tree they're bright green, like a green walnut hull, but not nearly as bitter. They are, however, more bitter in this state than they are when they dry out and turn brown. The nut meat is very fresh, however, and acts as a kind of counterbalance to the green hull. Hickory nuts are mild, only slightly perceptible in the finished beer. Pecans, of course, have the distinctive sweet aroma of baked bread and caramel.

Over time, as the hickory nut and its hull

sit on the ground, they dry out and harden, and the hull starts to naturally break apart in sections. More often than not we use the hull in this stage, when it's less bitter and slightly nuttier. Usually the squirrels will have gotten the nut meat by then, but the hulls retain quite a bit of flavor.

Bark

Bark from the shagbark hickory lives up to its name. It's easy to pull off because it hangs shaggily on the side of the tree, often coming off in 3- or 4-foot sections. Be careful not to pull bark that's firmly attached, because you could kill the tree. Once toasted, the bark gives off the most incredible sweet aroma of incense, toasted marshmallow, and campfire. When boiled in beer the flavor comes through remarkably well in the finished product. Bark can be harvested the day of brewing, or even weeks ahead of time. We often freeze bark if we're harvesting a lot but are not going to use it for some time. We feel this helps preserve its state as it comes off the tree. We do not, however, toast the bark before preserving it in any state as then it will rapidly lose the toasty incense-marshmallow flavor.

BREWING

Leaves

Leaves green or dried are a great bittering addition, added at 60 minutes before the end of the boil. Crush them up a little in your hands as you put them into a mesh bag. Use about a quarter pound for a 5-gallon batch.

Nuts

We use both the hickory hull and the nuts. As with all nuts, the hull contains similar flavor compounds as the nut, and since we're not restricted by our inability to chew through a hull in beer, we can utilize them for extra flavor. We boil the hulls for 60 minutes. Use a mesh bag so it's easy to pull them out, although allowing them to boil freely shouldn't obstruct your transfer later. A half pound of hulls in a 5-gallon batch will give light flavor.

The nuts themselves are more delicate. They can also be boiled for 60 minutes, but if you're able to collect a substantial amount of the nut meat, you'll get more flavor if you add them in the fermenter. We recommend chopping them roughly and toasting for 10 minutes, until they start to turn golden. Add them to the fermenter after they've cooled slightly. If you only use a small amount of nuts, you are better off adding them to the boil with the hulls. Pecans, however, being slightly more flavorful, will be best if added to the fermenter even if you have a relatively small amount. The oil is low in hickory nuts, and moderate in pecans. You may lose some head retention by adding to the fermenter.

Bark

To toast the bark, you will have best results toasting the same day or the day before you brew. Toast at about 350 degrees Fahrenheit for 30 to 45 minutes, until the smell of marshmallow is almost overwhelming and your bark is toasty brown but not black. Be

sure not to allow the bark to burn. Results will vary based on the time of year, the moisture in the bark, the temperature of your oven, and other factors.

In our first attempt, we boiled the bark for 60 minutes and had great results. Since then we've tried boiling for less time and adding

toasted bark to the fermenter; however, we found that the flavor is much less perceptible and even a little bit more bitter and woody when boiled for less time or just added to the fermenter. The best way to infuse the bark flavor is in a 60-minute boil addition. If you don't have a mesh bag large enough, the bark should be okay to add to the kettle freely in large pieces, as they shouldn't jam during your transfer. Use about 1½ pounds for a 5-gallon batch.

It may happen that you're not totally satisfied with the intensity of your bark character after fermentation. We've experienced this even while following our own guidelines to the letter, as there are often a number of uncontrollable variables at play like weather and moisture. To infuse more bark flavor, you can add more to the fermenter. Follow the guidelines for toasting and then add the bark pieces whole to your fermentation vessel. We taste after three days and then rack when the flavor is to our liking, which may take up to a couple of weeks. Consider transferring your beer to a secondary fermenter to rack off the yeast before adding the bark. If there is too much bark character, let the beer condition for a few months before drinking.

Finally, we've used both shagbark hickory and pecan bark to make syrups. We use the syrups for all kinds of things (pancakes for one), but these can also be added to the beer during the boil, or fermentation, or as a priming sugar. Making a syrup with the bark is also a good way to preserve the flavor if you don't want to keep big chunks of bark in your freezer. Use the same proportion of bark to water as we suggest for beer and add an equal amount of sugar to water, as if making a simple syrup. Boil everything for an hour on moderate heat with a lid on to keep from evaporating. We've tried making an alcoholic infusion with hickory bark, but have found that the alcohol brings out a lot of the bitterness and tannins in the bark—much more so than boiling—so making a syrup seems best for preserving and adding back to beer later.

PIGNUT

Batch Size: 5 gallons

OG: 1.062

FG: 1.013

ABV: 6.4%

Bitterness: 36 IBU

GRAINS

4 pounds 6 ounces Pilsner
3 pounds 12 ounces Vienna
3 pounds 8 ounces Munich

MASH

Mash in with 4½ gallons water to hit
    152 degrees Fahrenheit
Sparge with 7 gallons water at
    168 degrees Fahrenheit

HOPS

½ ounce Nugget at 60 minutes
½ ounce Hallertauer Mittelfrüh at
    30 minutes
½ ounce Fuggle at 20 minutes

ADDITIONAL INGREDIENTS

½ pound pignut hickory hulls at
    60 minutes
1 cup pignut hickory nuts toasted and
    added to fermenter

LENGTH OF BOIL

90 minutes with 15-minute whirlpool at
    flameout

YEAST

American Ale

FERMENTATION

*Ferment at 62 degrees Fahrenheit for
two weeks, then raise to 70 degrees until
fermentation is complete.*

*Add the remaining 1 cup of toasted pig-
nut hickory nuts to the fermenter and
condition for another two weeks.*

SHAGBARK 80 SHILLING

Batch Size: 5 gallons

OG: 1.050

FG: 1.014

ABV: 4.7%

Bitterness: 23 IBU

GRAINS

7 pounds 4 ounces Maris Otter

1 pound 4 ounces crystal 20°L

7 ounces Special B

6 ounces crystal 40°L

½ ounce pale chocolate malt

MASH

Mash in with 4 gallons water to hit 155 degrees Fahrenheit

Sparge with 6½ gallons water at 168 degrees Fahrenheit

HOPS

½ ounce Nugget at 60 minutes

ADDITIONAL INGREDIENTS

1½ pounds toasted hickory bark at 60 minutes

LENGTH OF BOIL

60 minutes with 15-minute whirlpool at flameout

YEAST

British Ale

FERMENTATION

Begin fermentation at 66 degrees Fahrenheit for two days and allow to rise a couple of degrees every day until it hits 75 degrees.

AMERICAN LOTUS

It is no surprise that the lotus has been associated with mystical, magical properties and been given a sacred place in numerous cultures for centuries. With its giant leaves and stalks, its inverted cone-shaped seed-pod, and the symmetry of its flower, it is a captivating aquatic plant that resembles almost no other plant in the world.

Many associate the sacred lotus (*Nelumbo nucifera*), native to much of Asia, with Hindu and Buddhist traditions, but the American lotus (*Nelumbo lutea*), native to

North America, has a long tradition among indigenous tribes, particularly of the Mississippi and Missouri River Valleys. Lotus tubers were eaten like potatoes and the seeds were eaten in both young and mature forms. The plant spread throughout most of the eastern portion of the United States as a result of being carried by different tribes. American lotus was traditionally found around flood plains but can now be found in swamps, ponds, lakes, marshes, and is often used as a decorative water plant. It is ubiquitous in some places and rarely seen in others; in Minnesota it is protected but in Rhode Island it is a nuisance—go figure. For those who cannot forage for lotus, the seeds and roots can often be found in Asian grocery stores. In theory, the root can be used like potatoes or other tubers to add extra fermentable sugar to the mash, although we haven't tried this ourselves. Check with local state regulations about harvesting American Lotus in your area.

HARVESTING

Flowers and Roots

The roots, leaves, flowers, and seeds of the American Lotus are edible. The flowers bloom in July and can be eaten like spinach. The roots can be harvested any time and grow under water, rooting into the shallow soil below. Digging the roots can be a chore. Native Americans would dig with their feet

and work them up out of the ground with a hooked pole. We've never brewed with the roots, but imagine they are similar to brewing with potatoes—starchy and good for the mash.

Seeds

The seeds have the most flavor for brewing and they're what we use most frequently from the plant. We harvest the seeds in the fall after the flowering period and before our waterways are too cold to navigate. During this time, the leaves will have withered and fallen back into the water, leaving only the dried seed pod 2 to 3 feet above water level. Waiting to harvest until cooler months also allows the seeds to drop out of their pods and re-seed in the water before collecting what's left, creating a sustainable harvest. It also gives the pods time to dry out so they'll be easier to crack when harvesting the seeds.

In order to harvest the seeds, cut off the seedpods and gather them in a 5-gallon bucket. Crack the pods with something heavy until everything falls to the bottom of the bucket. Pull out big pieces of the pod and keep cracking; however, you will inevitably be left with pod debris in addition to your seeds. You can "sift" the debris from the seeds by filling the bucket with water. The pod debris and hollow seeds will float to the top of the water while the good seeds will sink. You can skim the debris off the top of the water and collect what's left at the bottom. The seeds have the added benefit of being extremely easy to preserve. After harvesting from the seedpod, allow the seeds to air dry; they will keep whole in Mason jars for months before using.

BREWING

Flowers and Roots

With their leafy-green flavor and aroma, lotus flowers can work in conjunction with other herbs in an herbal tonic-type of beer. You might want to think of lotus blossoms as having similar uses to nettle and dandelion greens, as seen in earlier chapters. Add at various points during the boil in a mesh bag for a unique "green" flavor and aroma; just 1 pound in a 5-gallon batch in conjunction with other plants is sufficient.

Seeds

We like using lotus seeds in brewing, as they lend a special nuttiness that complements biscuity beers with a rich, bready malt character. For eating, the seeds must be hulled; for brewing, they can be toasted whole, or crushed and put directly into the boil or fermenter. We toast our seeds at about 450 degrees Fahrenheit. Keep an eye on the seeds as they toast; when they start to smell fragrant, after around 20 to 30 minutes, they're ready for use. If using whole, unhulled seeds, surround them with foil; this will keep them contained when they start to pop. Crack with a hammer when they come out. Add to the fermenter; they should fall to the bottom and you can rack above. Use about a half pint to a pint jar's worth of seeds for a 5-gallon batch.

LOTUS SEED BIÈRE DE GARDE

Batch Size: 5 gallons

OG: 1.065

FG: 1.014

ABV: 6.6%

Bitterness: 22 IBU

GRAINS
6 pounds Pilsner
5 pounds Munich
9 ounces crystal 60°L
9 ounces pale chocolate malt
4 ounces Special B

MASH
Mash in with 5 gallons water to hit
    147 degrees Fahrenheit
Sparge with 6½ gallons water at
    168 degrees Fahrenheit

HOPS
½ ounce Nugget at 60 minutes

ADDITIONAL INGREDIENTS
1 pint jar of roasted lotus seeds added to
    fermenter

LENGTH OF BOIL
90 minutes with 15-minute whirlpool at
    flameout

YEAST
German Alt

FERMENTATION
*Ferment at 56 degrees Fahrenheit for
two weeks, then allow to rise to
70 degrees until fermentation is complete.*

*Add the lotus seeds and condition for
another two weeks.*

OAK

In the Northern Hemisphere, we probably have a more profound relationship with oak than with any other tree. We live with it, in it, and on it. It shelters us during the summer in vast swaths of hardwood forest; it makes up our chairs, tables, dressers, and cabinets; it frames our homes and buildings; we've (historically) sailed on it; we entrust our cherished fermented drinks to its staves. Oak is sacred and hallowed and one of our most loyal companions. Our lives would be impoverished in look, feel, smell, and taste without it.

There are uses for just about every part of the oak tree, even multiple uses for each part. Each element of the oak adds dimensions to the complex flavor we recognize from barrels: tannin, vanilla, freshly cut wood, cinnamon. The bark has some of the spiciness; the acorns can be fermented to give unreal bourbon aromas; the leaves impart a bitter tannin quality; and oak heartwood houses the classic oak flavors and aromas we know so well. We could talk almost endlessly about its uses among Native Americans and so many other cultures in all parts of the Northern Hemisphere. Every part of the oak tree has been used for centuries for food, medicine, building—just about everything under the sun.

You don't need to spend a few hundred dollars on a barrel to infuse that unmistakable character. Barrels these days are in high demand and short supply, partly because people are looking to infuse the flavor of the wine or spirit that was previously in the barrel, but also partly because there are so many microbrewers, distillers, and wine-makers craving oak that coopers can hardly keep up. Fortunately for beer, you don't need a barrel; you just need a tree.

HARVESTING

Leaves

We use the leaves green in the summer, and brown after they've fallen off the tree in autumn. We find them to be some of the more bitter and tannic leaves we've used, which makes them great for bittering. If harvesting from the ground, the only thing you want to be sure of is that they are crisp and dry. Wet leaves can become moldy and don't have that fall leaf pile character you want to infuse into the beer. Red oak acorns are very tannic, and we assume that their leaves are also slightly more tannic and bitter than other species like white oak. Be aware of slight variations among species.

Wood

Unless you're chopping down a tree, you may not have immediate access to the wood. However, it is probably more readily available than you think. We have a number of storms that knock over trees in this part of the Midwest, so we always keep an eye out for fallen oaks. A lot of firewood is oak, too, so ask for oak at places that supply it. Any wood will keep for years when cut, and is sometimes even better over time as the tannins will leach out through rain and weather, so you can gather a lot at once and keep it over time. If you come upon someone who is cutting down an oak tree or trimming a tree, you can gather shavings, cuttings, or even a portion of the tree—it will last you a long time for homebrewing. If possible, store outside in a covered area to allow it to dry. Of course, the wood itself can also be procured from homebrew supply stores in the form of oak spirals and chips, usually pretoasted. It's also becoming common to see homebrew-size oak barrels, or for homebrew clubs to gather together for a big brew day to fill a full-size barrel.

Acorns

Acorns will litter the ground in the fall, although you have to be quick to get them before the animals do. They have been used for centuries for food, but first have to be leached of their bitter tannins to become edible. Below are two ways to do this. One is a common method, generally used to make acorn flour; the other is a little more unusual but makes incredible, unexpected flavors.

To leach the acorns of their tannins, you will first have to separate the acorn nut from the cap. It may be helpful to let the acorns age for some time before you separate the shell from the nut on the inside, anywhere from a week to several months. You should try to get as much of the brown skin off as

possible as it is one of the more bitter parts, like walnut skins. As with ginger, freezing the acorn before cracking helps get the skins off later. Put the nuts into a food processor with water in a ratio of about 1 part nuts to

2 parts water and purée until moderately smooth, like coarsely ground coffee. Add to a mason jar (as big as you need for the task—could be a half gallon or more) and

fill with water in about a $^{50}\!/\!_{50}$ ratio. Let sit in the fridge.

The leaching will take place over about a week. Pour off the top layer of water every day and add a new layer of water. Shake the contents and let sit in the fridge. You want the flour to be relatively tasteless in the end, not bitter at all. This will be different for every tree and every species of oak. Taste test starting after three days, and go for as many as 10 or more. Once the flour is neutral, dry it (a dehydrator is fastest, but you can let it sit out on paper towels). At this point, if you were cooking with the flour you would purée one more time until absolutely smooth, but for beer it's okay as-is. The flour will be best to add to the mash—there's even some starch in it that will convert to sugar.

The second way to process acorns is to ferment them. This is by far our favorite way, although it will require a lot more patience. For this method, just take the cap off the acorns and dry the nuts with the shell on. Put them in one layer on a baking sheet and let them sit out in dry weather. After about a week, put them in a mason jar, seal the jar, and let them be for a year. At that point you should start to smell rum, raisin, plum, bourbon, Madeira, all of the most amazing smells anyone could hope to get from oak.

BREWING

Leaves

Add the leaves at 60 minutes for bittering in a mesh bag. You will need about 8 ounces for a 5-gallon batch. They can replace about half the hops in a beer up to 25 IBUs; or use them entirely for your bittering addition for a low-bittered beer.

Wood

There are some old recipes for Oak Ale that call for boiling the bark for 45 minutes with the wort. This will most certainly extract tannins and can be used in place of a hop addition. Bark can also be added to the fermenter, although it won't be as classically aromatic as the wood itself. You can some-times pull bark off the side of a log that's been split for firewood.

We toast chunks of the oak heartwood in our oven at about 350 degrees Fahrenheit for 45 minutes or so. This not only kills anything that might be living on the wood, it also gives it a little char, a bit like one would find on the inside of the barrel. You can play around with your toasting method. A light toast will give a fresh-cut wood character; medium toast has more spicy cinnamon aromas; dark toast gives a richer vanillins. A combo of all three toasts can be quite nice. We add the wood to the fermenter like you would oak chips and let it sit until we like the character of the beer. This depends a lot on the wood, the toast, and the final effect we're going for; it could be anywhere from a week to a month or more. If letting the wood sit for a month, be sure to rack into a secondary fermenter first. Use about two 12-inch by 3-inch sections of oak heartwood for a 5-gallon batch.

Acorns

If using acorn flour, the flour can be added to the mash. It will add a hint of nuttiness to the finished product and a little tannin. Try about a pound for a 5-gallon batch and add about a quarter pound of rice hulls to make sure the mash doesn't stick.

If using fermented acorns, they can be added to the fermenter. We haven't run into any problems with unwanted wild yeast or bacterial infections at this stage, but in theory this could be a problem. A beer with a fair amount of alcohol that has already gone through its primary fermentation should help stave off the contamination to a certain degree. The flavor of the acorns should infuse quickly. Add a half-pint jar's worth of fermented acorns and check after a couple of days. Rack when the flavor is to your liking.

The recipe in this chapter comes from a series of beers we did in 2015 that were made with all different parts of a single tree (a couple other beers from that series appear in this book). We used leaves, bark, wood, sap, fruit, nuts, or other parts that made each tree distinctive in order to showcase the unique flavors of each. The oak beer in the series made use of the leaves, wood, acorns, and even black trumpet mushrooms that grow on or around oak. The recipe is a good overview of how to use each different part of the tree in the process. Feel free to mix and match when brewing this beer; omit some ingredients (like the fermented acorns or mushrooms), bump up the oak wood addi-tion, or add acorn flour.

SINGLE TREE: OAK

Batch Size: 5 gallons
OG: 1.052
FG: 1.012
ABV: 5.3%
Bitterness: 27 IBU

GRAINS

8 pounds Maris Otter
1 pound Victory
8 ounces crystal 40°L
8 ounces crystal 60°L
4 ounces black malt

MASH

Mash in with 4 gallons water to hit
151 degrees Fahrenheit
Sparge with 6½ gallons water at
168 degrees Fahrenheit

HOPS

½ ounce Nugget at 60 minutes
½ ounce East Kent Goldings at
15 minutes

ADDITIONAL INGREDIENTS

8 ounces oak leaves at 60 minutes
3 ounces dried black trumpet
mushrooms at 10 minutes
2 (12-inch by 3-inch-long) sections
oak heartwood, one medium toast
and one dark toast, added to the
fermenter
1 half-pint jar's worth of fermented
acorns, added to the fermenter

LENGTH OF BOIL

60 minutes with 15-minute whirlpool at
flameout

YEAST

British Ale

FERMENTATION

*Ferment at 64 degrees Fahrenheit for
two days, then allow to rise a couple
degrees every day until fermentation is
complete.*

*Add the fermented acorns and the
toasted oak heartwood after primary
fermentation is complete. Taste after
two days and rack when the flavor is to
your liking.*

AMERICAN PERSIMMON

Those living in the western half of the United States may not be aware that there is a native American persimmon tree that grows wild in our forests. Unless cultivated, the tree doesn't make its way farther west than Texas or Kansas. But in the eastern half of the United States, wild persimmons can grow in abundance and have been used for centuries by Native Americans.

The fruit of the American persimmon, or common persimmon, is a much different size and shape than the Japanese persimmon. Japanese persimmons are the world's most cultivated variety and are found in grocery stores across the country. They are much larger and have meatier flesh than American persimmons, which are quite small, usually no more than an inch or two in diameter, with a tough, woody skin and a mushy, pudding-like interior texture. American Persimmons are loaded with vitamin C and have a flavor more akin to bitter orange and peach, with a hint of cinnamon.

Persimmon has been an important fruit for Native American tribes like the Cherokee and Rappahannock. Not only was the fruit itself eaten and preserved, it was made into salves for medicinal purposes, and both the fruit and bark were brewed in teas. One mention of persimmon use as a beverage among the Rappahannock describes the fruit rolled in corn meal, brewed in water, drained, baked, and mixed with hot water to make a beer. As hard as this is to imagine, a recipe discovered by John T. Edge, the director of the Southern Foodways Alliance, and originally penned by an unknown Mississippi author, describes making a persimmon beer with similar ingredients to the Rappahannock delicacy. After lining a wooden barrel with corn shucks, the beer-maker is directed to mash persimmons, corn meal, and sweet potato peelings in the barrel, cover with water, and let stand until "the taste is right." The author recommends serving in a cup with corn bread. Persimmons and corn—a natural pair for these United States.

HARVESTING

American persimmons are astringent to an extreme when harvested before they're ripe, and some trees simply never develop a sufficiently sweet fruit. They should never be harvested from the tree, as they only become suitably ripe when they fall to the ground. They're also one of the prized fruits for forest animals, often eaten by deer and squirrels before you even see them on the ground. That's because deer and squirrels know better than to eat them off the tree! Some common advice suggests that you need to wait for a frost to harvest persimmons, but timing is relatively arbitrary. Each tree seems to be on its own timetable, and the only thing that really matters is that the fruit is on the ground. Like paw paws, persimmons also have a tendency to ferment quickly after falling to the ground, in part because the delicate fruit very often splits when it hits the ground. If a fruit smells like nail polish, don't bother collecting it. You're just asking to bring *Acetobacter* into your brewhouse. Persimmons also freeze well so you can harvest over a period of time, freeze, and then brew when you have enough.

BREWING

Persimmon skins are loaded with natural yeast and bacteria. In our experience, it's easy to infect a batch of beer with bacteria when using fresh persimmons in the fermenter. We solve this problem by adding persimmons to the end of the boil, or by adding to the fermenter after first bringing the pulp to at least 180 degrees Fahrenheit for 15 minutes or more in a pot or pan.

Pulp the persimmons the same way we recommend for paw paws in order to separate the bitter skin and seeds before adding to the boil or to the fermenter. If adding to the boil, a mesh bag will help keep some of the pulp from potentially clogging your transfer. You can add the pulp directly to the fermenter and let it fall to the bottom of your vessel before racking. Sugar and flavor of persimmons can vary from year to year and tree to tree. Start with a cup of pulp for a 5-gallon batch. You can add more later if you want more flavor.

If you don't have American persimmons near you, you can also use Japanese persimmons. Their flesh is slightly less flavorful, so you should use closer to 3 or more pounds of fruit for a 5-gallon batch. The spicebush berries we recommend in the Persimmon Spicebush Bière de Garde add a pepper- and clove-like complement to persimmon; we recommend spicebush berries, allspice berries, peppercorns, or cloves, especially to complement Japanese persimmons.

In general, we pair persimmons with Belgian yeast strains, but taking a cue from our friends in the southeast, we recommend trying a beer made with flaked maize or even mashed with corn bread!

PERSIMMON-SPICEBUSH BIÈRE DE GARDE

Batch Size: 5 gallons

OG: 1.065

FG: 1.014

ABV: 6.8%

Bitterness: 24 IBU

GRAINS

11 pounds 12 ounces Vienna

8 ounces Special B

4 ounces table sugar

MASH

Mash in with 4½ gallons water to hit
147 degrees Fahrenheit

Sparge with 7 gallons water at
168 degrees Fahrenheit

HOPS

½ ounce Columbus at 60 minutes

¼ ounce East Kent Goldings at
15 minutes

ADDITIONAL INGREDIENTS

1 cup persimmon pulp, added 5 minutes
before the end of the boil

2 tablespoons ground spicebush berries,
added 5 minutes before the end of the
boil (you can substitute with allspice
berries and/or peppercorns)

LENGTH OF BOIL

90 minutes with 15-minute whirlpool at
flameout

YEAST

German Alt

FERMENTATION

*Ferment at 58 degrees Fahrenheit for
two weeks, then allow to rise to
70 degrees until fermentation is
complete.*

APPLE

Nothing is as emblematic of industrial farming as the Red Delicious apple. Marika remembers unsuccessfully attempting to trade away Red Delicious apples that her father had sliced and put into her lunch bag during elementary school. For a long time she refused to eat apples at all. That bitter red skin and often mealy interior—it's certainly not a fruit to be kicked out of paradise over! The Red Delicious has been bred for over a hundred years for its color more than its flavor, as well as for the thick skin that allows it a longer shelf life. Thankfully consumer tastes changed in the late 1990s as new varieties, like Gala and Fuji, made their way to market and introduced refreshing flavors. Since then the Red Delicious has declined almost 40 percent in sales, and we're seeing a resurgence in interest in new and old varieties of apples with full and diverse flavors—even if they don't have that glossy lipstick exterior.

Southern Illinois orchards are filled with apples. Jonathon is a popular one: small and mottled red and yellow, it is sweet with a moderate punch of tartness. Pomona Winery, nested in the woods south of us, makes a beautiful dry Jonathon wine you could easily mistake for a grape wine. Jonathon is a variety that appears to have originated in New York State, most likely related to the Esopus Spitzenburg, an old variety thought to be a favorite of Thomas Jefferson. We have Esopus Spitzenburg in our garden, along with Honeycrisp, Cox's Orange Pippin, and Grimes Golden— one of Aaron's grandmother's favorites. Together they would make a nice blend for cider. In fact, as anyone who makes cider will tell you, a good cider is a balance of several varieties of apples, selected for their tannins, tartness, and a wisp of their unique honey sweetness. The best ciders are often bone dry, can be relatively still or effusively effervescent, and sometimes even a little funky—descriptors often associated with champagne and beer. The more you delve into the world of ciders, particularly from France or Spain, the more you'll realize the overlap the apple has with some of the flavors we love most about beer. With the resurgence of heirloom fruits, some of the thousands of historical varieties of apples are now becoming available again, so you can experiment with a large number of apples to pick out your favorites for tartness, fruitiness, or tannin.

Beers we've made with apples at Scratch have been a celebration of these historical qualities, as well as a celebration of autumn. One of our recipes included here is an attempt to mimic the tartness of cider, while the other imparts a smoky flavor to caramelized apples to create a fall beer that has been one of our all-time favorites. Although our recipes all call for fresh apples, feel free to use the methods of preservation below to substitute dried apple rings or juice, and see how it affects the character of the beer.

HARVESTING

When apples are ready to harvest, there are usually a *lot* to harvest. Fortunately, apples are also a great fruit to store and preserve. Certain varieties store better and longer than others, so it's best to consult a guide with information about specific apple varieties. In general, if kept in a cool (but not freezing) place, picked over for worms or other spots, given good air circulation, and kept away from onions, potatoes, or pears, many apples will keep for a couple months and some as many as five months.

Dried apple rings are another great way to preserve the harvest and can make an excellent addition to beer. Slice thin and dry in a dehydrator.

Finally, the juice of the apples can be frozen and stored indefinitely. Juicing takes more time, but for brewing it can also be a big benefit, as it will impart more apple character and more fermentable sugar into the mix.

You may not think you have room for a fruit tree in your yard, but you will be rewarded if you decide to plant one. Apple trees take a few years to really produce, but one tree will give you enough apples for several batches of beer or 5 gallons of cider. The flavor of your own apples from your own tree is also incomparable, like fresh tomatoes from your garden. If you have the space, it's worth it.

BREWING

As with so many other plants, a bruised apple or one you would otherwise turn into apple sauce because it's only half edible is a perfect candidate for beer. Cut off the bad parts and you're ready to go.

Like peaches, apple skins are also loaded with yeast and bacteria. We use a strategy for brewing with apples that's similar to our approach with peaches. First, we don't usually skin the apple—too much work. If the apples are going directly into the fermenter, we do submerge them in sanitizing solution to kill as much wild yeast and bacteria as possible. Very often we add fresh apples to the end of the boil to sterilize them. We seed them, quarter them, and chop them fine in a food processor to get as much surface area contact as possible. When making a sour beer, like the one included in this recipe, we are more game to put fresh apples into the fermenter. Note that most apples in this country are sprayed with some kind of pesticide, so it is very important to wash apples well before putting them into beer. Also, be sure to de-seed all apples since the seeds carry a compound that metabolizes into cyanide. Add 6 pounds for a 5-gallon batch.

We have also had great results puréeing the apples and cooking them for a long time, the same way one would make applesauce. This caramelizes the sugar in the apples and adds an extra layer of sweetness. We find little to no loss of apple character in the finished product, and this can go directly into the boil or fermenter without adverse effects from wild yeast and bacteria. We highly recommend this method for any apple addition, but especially for the smoked beer recipe included in this chapter. For a 5-gallon batch, puree 5 pounds of apples and cook down in a covered pot on medium until the apples fall apart and become brown and caramelized. Add a little water to the pot to keep the apples from burning.

SMOKED APPLE ALE

Batch Size: 5 gallons

OG: 1.055

FG: 1.011

ABV: 5.9%

Bitterness: ? IBU

GRAINS

6 pounds 8 ounces Vienna

2 pounds wheat

1 pound Munich

8 ounces smoked malt

2 ounces rice hulls

MASH

Mash in with 4 gallons water to hit 150 degrees Fahrenheit

Sparge with 6½ gallons water at 168 degrees Fahrenheit

HOPS

½ ounce Chinook at 60 minutes

ADDITIONAL INGREDIENTS

5 pounds apples, puréed and cooked down until rich and caramelly, like applesauce. Add to boil at 5 minutes. (Our original recipe calls for an ounce of dried hickory leaves at the beginning of the boil. If you have hickory leaves near you, feel free to add them and reduce the hop addition by half to enhance the crisp fall flavor of this beer.)

LENGTH OF BOIL

60 minutes with 15-minute whirlpool at flameout

YEAST

British Ale

FERMENTATION

Ferment at 58 degrees Fahrenheit for two weeks, then allow to rise to 70 degrees until fermentation is complete.

SOUR APPLE

Batch Size: 5 gallons
OG: 1.054
FG: 1.008
ABV: 6%
Bitterness: ? IBU

GRAINS
8 pounds Pilsner
2 pounds Munich

MASH
Mash in with 4 gallons water to hit
    147 degrees Fahrenheit
Sparge with 7½ gallons water at
    168 degrees Fahrenheit

HOPS
None

ADDITIONAL INGREDIENTS
6 pounds apples, seeded, cored,
    and puréed; add to end of boil at
    5 minutes

LENGTH OF BOIL
60 minutes with 15-minute whirlpool at
    flameout

YEAST
Mixed Culture

FERMENTATION
We ferment this beer with our sour-dough culture, which is a mix of Saccharomyces *and* Lactobacillus. *We pitch the culture at around 100 degrees Fahrenheit and hold it there for the first day. Berliner Weisse blends from several of the major yeast suppliers would approximate our culture. Follow the guidelines for fermentation temperature on these yeasts.*

SQUASH

We at Scratch are not big fans of pumpkin beer. I think it's safe to say we hate it. That's because the dirty truth is that most pumpkin beer is not brewed with pumpkin at all, but with a heavy dose of spices we associate with pumpkin pie and something orange and starchy that has more flavor, like other squash, yams, or sweet potatoes.

Every year we have rebelled against the pumpkin pie seasonal beer trend by brewing with the last thing anyone would expect: the seeds. Also known as *pepitas* (and affectionately referred to as "the *pepita* beer" by some of our regulars), roasted pumpkin seeds are a Mexican staple in the fall that have a fantastically aromatic toasted nuttiness.

Some forget that pumpkin is also a kind of squash, and therefore should display the rich variety of flavors of its culinary cousins; however, the pumpkin we most often see around Halloween has been bred over the years to stand up to carving, not to eating, and has suffered a loss of flavor. This is one reason why it is so often *not* used as a flavor ingredient in food that purportedly bears its name. But pumpkin, like all squash, contains layers of flavors and a variety of uses. From the pulp to the seeds, squash can be used as a fermentable ingredient in the mash and for flavoring in the boil and fermenter.

HARVESTING

Pulp

Squash is available in the fall but has the added benefit of being easily stored through the winter, and varieties of winter squash are equally good for brewing. You should experiment with different varieties to find out what you like best about each. Very often we blend three or four types together. Some can be bland or a little too vegetal. It helps to taste the squash before putting it in beer so you can decide how to adjust. Every harvest will be a little different.

Squash is a hardy gourd that can also be cellared so you can hold onto it after the fall for use in colder months. Bigger squash are also easier to process, but there's more flavor in smaller gourds. When looking for squash to grow, planting varieties that store well will allow you to utilize the ingredient later in the year. Butternut and acorn squash are two kinds that will keep well through the winter.

The easiest way to pulp squash is to cut it in half and de-seed it, then roast it facedown in an oven at 450 degrees Fahrenheit for 45 minutes. When it feels soft when poked with a fork, take it out of the oven and scoop the insides out with a spoon.

Seeds

You can harvest the seeds at the same time you're preparing the squash for the oven.

Scoop them out and rinse off the fibers as best you can, then allow them to dry. You can then toast them in the oven at 450 degrees Fahrenheit until they turn golden and start to pop.

BREWING

Pulp

We've found roasting effective particularly for squashes like pumpkin, since the pulp itself is often mild and caramelizing it draws out hidden flavors in the sugars. Roasted squash pulp will give a little extra body and even a touch of butteriness, but can also verge on giving unwanted vegetal flavors, so be careful about adding too much. In general, roasting before adding pulp to the beer serves to moderate the vegetal flavors. We've added the pulp both to the end of the boil and to the fermenter with good results.

You can do a couple things with the pulp once you've pulled it from the skin of the gourd. You can either put it in the mash to try to extract the sugars and a little bit of color, or you can put it in the fermenter.

To add the squash pulp to the mash, you can take it directly from the oven and put it into your mash tun with your grains. Use about a pound for a 5-gallon batch, and consider adding about a quarter pound of rice hulls to keep the mash from sticking.

When we put the pulp in the fermenter, we like to roast it a little longer to caramelize more of the natural sugars. This helps render more flavor and aroma, and can give an extra hint of caramel and, surprisingly, a toasty breadiness. To do this, we roast the pulp taken from the gourd until most of it is golden brown. Alternatively, we skin the squash before putting it in the oven and then roast the cubes until they caramelize. The latter option is a little more work, but it creates more surface area to caramelize from the outset, and you don't have to touch it from when it comes out of the oven to when it goes into your fermenter (although we haven't run into problems skinning it after it comes out of the oven).

When the pulp comes out of the oven, place it in a mesh bag and add it to the kettle the last five minutes of the boil. If adding to a fermenter, it should sink to the bottom so you can rack above.

Seeds

We've toasted both hulled and unhulled pumpkin seeds for our Pumpkin Seed Ale and have found the results to be quite similar. (You can use seeds from any squash, not just pumpkin, so don't limit yourself in case you have different varieties of squash in the fall or winter.) We chop the seeds roughly in a food processor first to increase the surface area, then toast at 350 degrees Fahrenheit for 30 minutes. Keep an eye on the seeds to ensure that they don't burn; you may have to turn them several times before they're done cooking. Add about 10 ounces of toasted seeds to the fermenter after primary fermentation is complete.

SASSQUASH

Batch Size: 5 gallons

OG: 1.055

FG: 1.010

ABV: 5.9%

Bitterness: 37 IBU

GRAINS
5 pounds 8 ounces Vienna
3 pounds Munich
2 pounds Pilsner

MASH
Mash in with 5 gallons water to hit
149 degrees Fahrenheit
Sparge with 7 gallons water at
168 degrees Fahrenheit

HOPS
½ ounce Millennium at 60 minutes
1 ounce Willamette at 10 minutes

ADDITIONAL INGREDIENTS
1 teaspoon crushed black peppercorns
at 60 minutes
1 quart dried sassafras leaves at
5 minutes (substitute with filé spice—
which is made from sassafras leaves
and is safrole free—or spicebush
leaves)
1 quart roasted and puréed squash,
added in fermenter

LENGTH OF BOIL
90 minutes with 15-minute whirlpool at
flameout

YEAST
American Ale

FERMENTATION
*Begin fermentation at 68 degrees
Fahrenheit until fermentation is nearly
complete, then raise above 70 degrees
until finished.*

*Add the roasted squash after primary
fermentation is complete. Check flavor
after two days and rack when it is to
your liking.*

PUMPKIN SEED ALE

Batch Size: 5 gallons
OG: 1.052
FG: 1.012
ABV: 5.4%
Bitterness: 27 IBU

GRAINS
6 pounds Maris Otter
1 pound 12 ounces Munich
1 pound 8 ounces Vienna
8 ounces crystal 20°L

MASH
Mash in with 5 gallons water to hit
    149 degrees Fahrenheit
Sparge with 7 gallons water at
    168 degrees Fahrenheit

HOPS
½ ounce Columbus at 60 minutes
½ ounce East Kent Goldings at flameout

ADDITIONAL INGREDIENTS
10 ounces toasted pumpkin seeds,
    added to the fermenter

LENGTH OF BOIL
60 minutes with 15-minute whirlpool at
    flameout

YEAST
British Ale

FERMENTATION
Ferment at 67 degrees Fahrenheit until nearly complete, then raise temperature to 70 degrees until finished.

Add the pumpkin seeds after primary fermentation is complete. Check flavor after one day and rack when beer is to your preference.

HORSERADISH

Horseradish is certainly one of the most unusual plants for beer-making that you will find in this book. In the same family as mustard and wasabi, it is a plant with a burning spiciness that can bring you to tears. A bit like chili peppers in this way, everybody's threshold will be a little bit different, so start low and build up your additions to decide how you prefer it. Also like chili peppers, a mild to moderate addition will de-emphasize heat and instead bring out some of the other subtle flavors in the plant.

Everyone is familiar with horseradish roots grated and mashed with vinegar, often eaten as a sauce or spread. This tradition came out of Germany; it spread to England and other parts of Europe by the time of the Renaissance, and we still associate it with German food today. However, horseradish is an ancient cultivar, and well before this use caught on, the entire plant was used in a more holistic sense. The greens and the root were used for medicine, both through ingestion and topical use (to cure freckles, according to Maude Grieve). The greens, like so many others in this book, have a wonderful bitterness, much milder than the root, which can be used in salads as much as for bittering beer.

Today the horseradish capital of the world is in Collinsville, a town in southern Illinois near St. Louis. The farmland there and in the surrounding counties is part of the Mississippi River basin, fed by nutrients from the river. Soil in the region is rich in potassium, which enhances the spiciness of the horseradish, making it an ideal place for growing.

We use the whole plant in very moderate amounts. It gives a special mustard-like spicy bitterness and we have found it especially interesting with roasted malts in darker beers. Our Horseradish Stout recipe finishes a little sweet and chocolatey, and the horseradish cuts through nicely to enhance the coffee character of the malts. Horseradish is also a good green for blending with a handful of others for gruits or even just as an accompaniment to hops for a *je ne sais quoi* bitterness that's just different enough from hop bitterness that it actually helps to enhance the hop.

HARVESTING

The horseradish plant is usually harvested sometime after the first frost, once the greens have grown to enormous heights and the root to often enormous lengths. It is a plant that will survive a couple of years underground as well, growing larger with each season. For the purposes of brewing, since we use such a small amount, we actually prefer to harvest it a little earlier, around mid to late summer, when the greens are large and the root a more moderate length. This seems to create a better balance of bitterness and spice that we prefer in the finished beer. We harvest the whole plant, green and root, at the same time for brewing.

If you don't grow horseradish yourself and don't know anyone who does, it may be hard to get your hands on the root with greens. We simply don't eat the greens today, so most people don't consider them a food product, although they're not unlike beet greens or turnip greens. If you know a farmer at a farmers' market who grows horseradish, ask them to supply you with the greens one week. If you can't find the greens at all, the root will be fine on its own.

BREWING

We usually break the greens up roughly in our hands before putting them in a mesh bag to boil. Boil for 60 minutes. Use only an ounce for a 5-gallon batch in combination with a low bittering hop addition, about half the hops you would normally use for a beer up to about 25 IBUs.

Horseradish root is grated before use in food applications. This is because grating helps open the cells that contain enzymes that will break down into mustard oils in the presence of water. When making horseradish for food, however, vinegar is added almost immediately to help moderate the spiciness. Without this addition in beer, we may be left with something a bit too spicy if we finely grate the root. We usually chop the root and pulse it in the food processor a few times, finding that this helps to moderate the spiciness. You can play with any of these techniques in your brewing to bump up or down the spice according to your preference. Use the root in the boil immediately after breaking it up, placing it into a mesh bag and adding at 60 minutes. We use a combination of greens and root, using only an ounce of greens and an ounce of the root for a 5-gallon batch.

HORSERADISH STOUT

Batch Size: 5 gallons

OG: 1.064

FG: 1.014

ABV: 6.6%

Bitterness: 29 IBU

GRAINS

8 pounds 8 ounces Maris Otter

1 pound 4 ounces rye

1 pound chocolate malt

12 ounces crystal 80°L

8 ounces roasted barley

6 ounces Special B

MASH

Mash in with 5 gallons water to hit
148 degrees Fahrenheit

Sparge with 6 gallons water at
168 degrees Fahrenheit

HOPS

½ ounce Nugget at 60 minutes

ADDITIONAL INGREDIENTS

1 ounce leaves and 1 ounce root,
chopped and boiled for 60 minutes

LENGTH OF BOIL

60 minutes with 15-minute whirlpool at
flameout

YEAST

British Ale

FERMENTATION

*Ferment at 67 degrees Fahrenheit until
nearly complete, then raise temperature
to 70 degrees until finished.*

BURDOCK

"Though growing in its wild state hardly any animal except the ass will browse on this plant, the stalks, cut before the flower is open and stripped of their rind, form a delicate vegetable when boiled, similar in flavour to Asparagus."

— Maude Grieve, *A Modern Herbal*

Grieve's observation might apply to more than one plant in this book—stinging nettle is probably another good candidate. Burdock, from the thistle group, produces a flower whose involucre (ring of bracts below the petals), at its base, is covered in prickly hooks or burrs which have a tendency to cling to anything they touch. In fact, they were the inspiration for Velcro (in German the word "Klettverschluss" for Velcro literally means "burdock fastener"). And it's not a particularly glamorous plant, growing as it does in waste places. But it is a plant with a long history of use in Asia and Europe, and later in the United States.

Burdock root is most often used in cooking, although its leaves and seeds have also been used historically for medicinal purposes. The roots, unlike many of the other roots and tubers we explore in this book, are not especially bitter. They have a sweeter, potato-like flavor, and when fresh a sometimes slimy effect. Some well-established burdock plants have roots that grow as deep as a foot or two, and can be an inch thick.

The leaves are bitterer, akin to dock (the suffix of the word "burdock" shows its perceived relationship with dock), and as big as the biggest rhubarb leaves—although the leaves are non-toxic and edible, unlike rhubarb. They make a good bittering addition like dock, dandelion, horseradish, and arugula. We have never used the seeds in beer, but they have been used topically in homeopathic tinctures to treat skin diseases, and ingested to stave off dropsy and kidney afflictions, among other things.

Roasted burdock root has a deeply earthy coffee-like character which has given us great results in darker amber beers, porters, and rauchbier—the burdock root was noticeable even through a moderately heavy smoked-malt grain bill. This difficult plant, like stinging nettle, has a lot to give if you can harvest it without too much frustration!

HARVESTING

Root

Burdock root is usually harvested in the fall, often when the flowers have gone and the burr is still up. The roots can be quite long, so to harvest from the wild, a long shovel or other digging implement is best to get deep into the soil and pull up the whole root. You can use the root fresh, or dry it and save for later use. We usually roast the root because it brings out the earthiness a little bit more. Drying it first helps with the roasting process. Burdock has become popular in food in the United States, so it's becoming more widely available here. International grocery stores are a good place to find it if you don't grow it yourself or know someone who does.

Leaves

The leaves of the plant can be harvested at any time. They will get quite large, so it's more efficient to wait until late summer. They should be used fresh like dandelion or dock leaves.

BREWING

Root

To roast the root, chop it into 1- to 2-inch pieces and put it in an oven at 350 degrees Fahrenheit for about half an hour. You can roast it fresh or dry; if fresh, plan on it taking a little bit longer to roast. Keep an eye on the root in the oven, and pull it out when it starts to look like dark chocolate brown. The pieces can go into the boil or the fermenter directly, or ground to a powder. Our best results have come from adding the root to both the end of the boil and to the fermenter. When adding to the boil, use a mesh bag; when adding to the fermenter, simply drop them in as-is. They should fall to the bottom and you can rack above. Use about 3 ounces of toasted root for a 5-gallon batch.

Leaves

The leaves can be used for bittering. If they're particularly big, chop them up into smaller pieces first. Put them in a mesh bag and boil for 60 minutes with about a pound of greens per 5-gallon batch.

BURDOCK RAUCHBIER

Batch Size: 5 gallons
OG: 1.052
FG: 1.012
ABV: 5.2%
Bitterness: 23 IBU

GRAINS
4 pounds 12 ounces Munich
4 pounds 4 ounces German smoked malt
12 ounces crystal 40°L
4 ounces chocolate malt

MASH
Mash in with 4½ gallons water to hit 153 degrees Fahrenheit
Sparge with 6 gallons water at 168 degrees Fahrenheit

HOPS
1 ounce Fuggle at 60 minutes

ADDITIONAL INGREDIENTS
3 ounces burdock root, toasted until darker, not charred. (Weight is post-toast.) Grind up and add at 20 minutes. Use a mesh bag if the root is in large chunks; add straight if it's in a powder.

LENGTH OF BOIL
60 minutes with 15-minute whirlpool at flameout

YEAST
British Ale

FERMENTATION
Ferment at 67 degrees Fahrenheit until nearly complete, then raise temperature to 70 degrees until finished.

GINGER

More than likely, the supermarket ginger you have seen and used is cured, with a layer of brown skin and a tough, juicy, yellow interior. This ginger, native to Asia, is the ginger that became exported all over the world, is used extensively in many forms of Asian and Indian cuisines, and made its way west to Greece, Rome, and to Great Britain. In North America, wild ginger is a native plant that, although not actually related to Asian ginger, has a similar flavor that tends to be earthier, and is used in similar applications to its Asian counterpart. Nothing can quite replace the peculiar spicy, hot, even citrusy flavor of ginger.

You may not, however, have seen fresh ginger at your local farmers' market. Fresh ginger, straight out of the ground, is off-white with beautiful purple and green stems. It is spicy and has a remarkably fruity aroma that seems to die as it ages. However, it is not grown widely in the United States. We are lucky to have one intrepid nearby farm (read more about them in the next section on turmeric) experimenting with growing ginger and turmeric, and have been able to brew with ginger fresh from the ground.

Ginger was used extensively in Britain for beer, although that drink was usually made with ginger, water, and sugar, and was not malt-based. Interestingly, it was fermented with what was called Ginger Beer Plant, which was not a "plant" at all, but a mixed culture of *Saccharomyces* yeast and *Lactobacillus*. Ginger Beer Plant fell out of favor when *Saccharomyces* yeast became more widely available. It was saved by a German yeast bank, and is now available from suppliers for home use.

The lesson we can take from this bit of history is that once upon a time, ginger beer was a much more tart drink than what we know today, primarily because of the *Lactobacillus*. Our ginger beer recipe is malt-based, but takes on the tart character of the historical drink. It is low gravity, fermented dry with tart lemon notes from a mixed fermentation culture and a healthy dose of ginger spiciness.

In *Sacred and Herbal Healing Beers*, Stephen Harrod Buhner remarks that ginger stimulates peripheral circulation of the blood, making it an equally satisfying winter drink which has the effect of warming fingers and toes. We use ginger often in combination with other plants, and recommend it in winter warmers. We also include a recipe for a much maltier beer with other herbs and spices for colder seasons.

HARVESTING

If you're lucky to have a farmer near you who grows ginger, you may ask them to bring you a root fresh from the ground. You will immediately notice a difference, particularly in the aroma.

Ginger prefers hot, humid climates, so

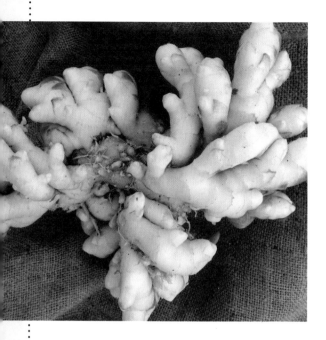

in water overnight and then plant them in a loose bed of sphagnum moss or coconut fiber, with the tips pointing up. The moss should be damp and allowed to dry before moistening again.

When you see green leaves forming the ginger is ready to plant in potting soil in a larger pot. Plant the ginger under just enough soil to cover the top of the rhizome. Ginger doesn't need a lot of direct sunlight; it just needs to stay warm and slightly humid. Ease it into the sun and spray it with water to keep moist. Start it inside in the spring and move it outside in the summer. It should be ready to harvest by the fall when temperatures start to drop.

not everyone's region is right for growing year-round; however, you can grow ginger yourself as a potted plant, moving it inside during cold months and outside during warm months. You can plant ginger straight from the grocery store (as long as it's not too dry), since ginger is itself a rhizome. If possible, pick a root that already has green tips. You may plant it as-is, or cut the ginger into 1- or 2-inch sections with a node, and sprout each individually. Soak the ginger pieces

BREWING

You can make ginger go a long way by chopping it finely to allow more surface area contact. The nice thing about using ginger in brewing is that it doesn't need to be peeled before use. We've found the easiest way to process it for brewing is to cut it roughly into 2- or 3-inch chunks and put it in a food processor until it's chopped finely. Put it in a large hop bag and boil for 60 minutes. Use 1½ pounds for a 5-gallon batch.

GINGER BEER

Batch Size: 5 gallons

OG: 1.042

FG: 1.003

ABV: 5%

Bitterness: ? IBU

GRAINS
3 pounds 4 ounces Munich
3 pounds 4 ounces Maris Otter
12 ounces table sugar

MASH
Mash in with 3 gallons water to hit
147 degrees Fahrenheit
Sparge with 7 gallons water at
168 degrees Fahrenheit

HOPS
None

ADDITIONAL INGREDIENTS
1½ pounds ginger, chopped in a food
processor, in boil at 60 minutes

LENGTH OF BOIL
60 minutes with 15-minute whirlpool at
flameout

YEAST
Mixed culture

FERMENTATION
*We ferment this beer with a sourdough
culture that is composed primarily of
Saccharomyces and Lactobacillus. We
pitch at around 100 degrees Fahrenheit
and let it go. You can use a sourdough
culture as well, or choose a commer-
cially available mixed culture with
Saccharomyces and Lactobacillus.*

*Alternatively, if you prefer something
dry but not sour, use a high-attenuating
Belgian Saison yeast.*

WINTER WARMER

Batch Size: 5 gallons
OG: 1.067
FG: 1.013
ABV: 7.2%
Bitterness: 30 IBU

GRAINS
7 pounds Maris Otter
5 pounds Munich
8 ounces crystal 80°L
8 ounces chocolate malt
4 ounces Special B

MASH
Mash in with 5 gallons water to hit
    148 degrees Fahrenheit
Sparge with 6 gallons water at
    168 degrees Fahrenheit

HOPS
½ ounce Nugget at 60 minutes
1 ounce Saaz at 10 minutes
1 ounce Saaz at flameout

ADDITIONAL INGREDIENTS
¾ pound ginger, chopped in a food
    processor, in boil at 60 minutes
2 tablespoons spicebush berries
    (substitute with allspice and/or
    peppercorns) at 60 minutes
2 (12-inch-long) spicebush branches at
    60 minutes
2 (12-inch-long) green cedar tips at
    60 minutes
1 sprig fresh lavender at 60 minutes
2 grams dried sage at 60 minutes

LENGTH OF BOIL
60 minutes with 15-minute whirlpool at
    flameout

YEAST
British Ale

FERMENTATION
*Ferment at 66 degrees Fahrenheit for
a week, then raise to 70 degrees until
primary fermentation is complete.*

TURMERIC

The first beer we brewed with turmeric was a Belgian tripel. We were familiar with the powdered version of the root from Indian and Southeast Asian cooking, although we had never used the whole root. But we lucked out: our friends Kris and Adriane had grown an experimental crop of turmeric at their farm, and while not native to southern Illinois (not even remotely—it grows best in year-round 68 to 85 degree Fahrenheit climates), it reminded us of several plants that do grow well here: spicebush and ginger.

We smelled the root; we tasted it; we turned it into tea. It was peppery and spicy like spicebush, with a familiar ginger snap. (Turmeric is a member of the ginger family, so it is no wonder that its flavor is similar.) We processed the whole batch and threw it into the boil the way we do with ginger, and the results were impressive. After fermentation we were left with a bright Belgian-style beer that had a profoundly earthy spiciness, not unlike the wild ginger that grows here. But it also had a black pepper and curry-like finish familiar from turmeric's culinary uses. We loved it.

Unlike the powder, fresh turmeric is more orange than yellow, and in spite of its spiciness it can also taste surprisingly similar to carrots. It's an incredibly versatile root that works well on its own and in combination with other plants.

HARVESTING

Turmeric leaves are often used in cooking, and theoretically could be used in beer, although we have not experimented with them that way yet. It is similar to ginger, harvested at the end of a long growing season. It can also be cured the same way as ginger, generally around 65 degrees Fahrenheit with 65 percent humidity, although it's much easier for our purposes and probably for yours, simply to freeze it if you can get it fresh.

BREWING

Chop the root into 1-inch chunks and process in a food processor until finely chopped. Put the chopped turmeric in mesh bags and boil for 30 minutes.

Since most people probably won't be able to find fresh turmeric near them, the easiest alternative is to use powdered turmeric. We would suggest trying 1 ounce of powdered turmeric, boiled for 30 minutes. The flavor of turmeric can be powerful upon packaging in kegs and bottles, so, if it is especially prominent, let it sit for several months before drinking. We let our Turmeric Tripel sit for 5 or 6 months before serving.

EXPERIMENTAL FARMING

Kris Pirmann and Adriane Koontz are two farmers who, like many young people, are coming back to cultivate the land. After gaining a wealth of experience around the United States growing diversified vegetables and working with dairy animals, the two settled down on their own farm in southern Illinois, and took to growing experimental crops that have either not been grown in the area for a long time, or have perhaps never been cultivated regionally at all.

Turmeric and ginger are two plants native to tropical climates, loaded with beneficial health properties, but not typically—rarely ever—grown in Illinois. Paying close attention to heat and humidity in their high tunnels, Kris and Adriane spent nine months nurturing their turmeric. They needed to keep it above 55 degrees Fahrenheit, which can be a challenge in southern Illinois, where we often get a late frost. One good thing about growing here, however, is that there aren't any of the pests normally adapted to tropical climates. And thankfully turmeric and ginger are not as intensive or demanding as lettuces and salad mixes. They may need a little love, but turmeric and ginger turn out to be quite manageable here, and we consumers get extra spiciness and fruitiness from a fresh harvest, plus all of the attendant health benefits.

Considering the exotic nature of ginger and turmeric, it seems like less of a stretch to grow a crop that was grown here for centuries and then forgotten. Kris and Adriane will be embarking with us on a multi-year project to grow barley, wheat, rye, spelt, and other grains which, with some exceptions, have not been grown here in a long time. It is difficult to grow barley in this relatively warm climate (too cold for ginger, too warm for grain), so we don't know how successful this endeavor will be. Also working against us has been the recent prevalence of blight in wheat and barley, making many grains in this area unusable for beer, food, or even for animals. With all of these factors at play, it takes the dogged initiative of young people who are willing to spend years working with the land to bring crops back to life. Not only does it take perseverance, it requires developing a re-acquaintance with the plants and how they interact with land and the weather over time. We see this endeavor with Kris and Adriane as a research partnership that can yield returns for other farmers and consumers in our area, and a model for farming in small communities anywhere in the country, where farmers, businesses, and consumers work in concert with one another as part of a symbiotic community.

TURMERIC TRIPEL

Batch Size: 5 gallons
OG: 1.074
FG: 1.006
ABV: 8.9%
Bitterness: 29 IBU

GRAINS
7 pounds Pilsner
3 pounds Vienna
1 pound 12 ounces table sugar
1 pound flaked oats

MASH
Mash in with 6 gallons water to hit
    150 degrees Fahrenheit
Sparge with 6 gallons water at
    168 degrees Fahrenheit

HOPS
½ ounce Columbus at 60 minutes
½ ounce Cluster at 20 minutes

ADDITIONAL INGREDIENTS
1 pound turmeric root finely diced at
    60 minutes

LENGTH OF BOIL
90 minutes with a 15-minute whirlpool
    at flameout

YEAST
Belgian Abbey Ale

FERMENTATION
*Ferment at 68 degrees Fahrenheit for
two days, then let rise to 80 degrees
naturally.*

REFERENCES

These are a selection of books we recommend or consult frequently for information on brewing with plants, as well as for information on identification and other uses of cultivated and wild plants. There are more books focused on other regions of the United States, perhaps closer to where you live, but these will give a good overview of most plants and historical brewing practices.

....

BREWING RESOURCES

Daniels, Ray. *Designing Great Beers.* Boulder: Brewers Publications, 2000.

Hieronymus, Stan. *Brew Like a Monk: Trappist, Abbey, and Strong Belgian Ales and How to Brew Them.* Boulder: Brewers Publications, 2005.

Markowski, Phil. *Farmhouse Ales: Culture and Craftsmanship in the Belgian Tradition.* Boulder: Brewers Publications, 2004.

Mosher, Randy. *Radical Brewing.* Boulder: Brewers Publications, 2004.

Palmer, John J. *How to Brew: Ingredients, Methods, Recipes, and Equipment for Brewing Beer at Home.* Boulder: Brewers Publications, 2006.

Papazian, Charlie. *The Complete Joy of Home Brewing, 3rd edition.* New York: Harper Collins, 2003.

BREWING WITH PLANTS

Arnold, John P. *Origin and History of Beer and Brewing.* Chicago: Alumni Association of the Wahl-Henius Institute of Fermentology, 1911.

Buhner, Stephen Harrod. *Sacred and Herbal Healing Beers.* Boulder: Brewers Publications, 1998.

Cornell, Martyn. *Amber, Gold & Black: The History of Britain's Great Beers.* Stroud, Gloucestershire: The History Press, 2010.

Fisher, Joe, and Dennis Fisher. *The Homebrewer's Garden.* Massachusetts: Storey Publishing, 1998.

Hieronymus, Stan. *Brewing Local.* Boulder: Brewers Publications, 2016.

Nordland, Odd. *Brewing and Beer Traditions in Norway: The Social Anthropological Background of the Brewing Industry.* Norway: The Norwegian Research Council for Science and the Humanities, 1969.

ON CULTIVATED AND WILD PLANTS

Elias, Thomas, and Peter Dykeman. *Edible Wild Plants: A North American Field Guide to Over 200 Natural Foods.* New York: Sterling, 2009.

Erichsen-Brown, Charlotte. *Medicinal and Other Uses of North American Plants: A Historical Survey with Special Reference to the Eastern Indian Tribes.* New York: Dover Publications, 1979.

Foster, Steven, and James A. Duke. *Peterson Field Guide to Medicinal Plants and Herbs of Eastern and Central North America.* New York: Houghton Mifflin Harcourt, 2014.

Grieve, Maude. *A Modern Herbal.* New York: Harcourt Brace and Company, 1931.

Hutchens, Alma R. *Indian Herbology of North America.* Boston: Shambhala Publications, 1973.

Kallas, John. *Edible Wild Plants: Wild Foods from Dirt to Plate.* Utah: Gibbs Smith, 2010.

Kindscher, Kelly. *Edible Wild Plants of the Prairie: An Ethnobotanical Guide.* Lawrence: University Press of Kansas, 1987.

Kindscher, Kelly. *Medicinal Wild Plants of the Prairie: An Ethnobotanical Guide.* Lawrence: University Press of Kansas, 1992.

Lincoff, Gary. *The Complete Mushroom Hunter: An Illustrated Guide to Finding, Harvesting, and Enjoying Wild Mushrooms.* Massachusetts: Quarry Books, 2010

Medseger, Oliver Perry. *Edible Wild Plants: The Complete, Authoritative Guide to Identification and Preparation of North American Edible Wild Plants.* New York: Collier Books, 1939.

Moerman, Daniel E. *Native American Ethnobotany.* Portland: Timber Press, 1998.

Tucker, Arthur O., and Thomas Debaggio. *The Encyclopedia of Herbs: A Comprehensive Reference to Herbs.* Portland: Timber Press, 2009.

RECIPE CONVERSIONS FOR EXTRACT BREWERS

Cedar IPA (page 9)

Put 11 ounces of crushed crystal 40°L into a grain bag to steep in 6½ gallons of water. Raise the temperature to 170 degrees Fahrenheit in about half an hour (if it comes to 170 more quickly, turn off heat and allow grains to steep for half an hour). Remove grain bag and bring to a boil. Slowly stir in 9 pounds of pale or Maris Otter liquid malt extract and boil for 60 minutes. Follow the hop and other ingredient schedules as outlined in the recipe.

Sahti (page 10)

Put 10 ounces of chocolate malt and 4 ounces of Special B into a grain bag to steep in 6½ gallons of water. Raise the temperature to 170 degrees Fahrenheit in about half an hour (if it comes to 170 more quickly, turn off heat and allow grains to steep for half an hour). Remove grain bag and bring to a boil. Slowly stir in 9 pounds of liquid rye malt extract and boil for 60 minutes. Follow the hop and other ingredient schedules as outlined in the recipe.

Wild Grapevine Wee Heavy (page 17)

Put 4 ounces of crushed crystal 80°L and 4 ounces of crushed roasted barley into a grain bag to steep in 6½ gallons of water. Raise the temperature to 170 degrees Fahrenheit in about half an hour (if it comes to 170 more quickly, turn off heat and allow grains to steep for half an hour). Remove grain bag and bring to a boil. Slowly stir in 9 pounds of pale liquid malt extract and 1 pound of amber liquid malt extract and boil for 60 minutes. Follow the hop and other ingredient schedules as outlined in the recipe.

Rose Root Bière de Mars (page 21)

Put 11 ounces of crushed Special B and 1 ounce of black malt into a grain bag to steep in 7 gallons of water. Raise the temperature to 170 degrees Fahrenheit in about half an hour (if it comes to 170 more quickly, turn off heat and allow grains to steep for half an hour). Remove grain bag and bring to a boil. Slowly stir in 7 pounds 11 ounces of Pilsner liquid malt extract and 1 pound of amber liquid malt extract and boil for 90 minutes. Follow the hop and other ingredient schedules as outlined in the recipe.

Sweet Potato Vienna (page 24)

You won't have a mash turn to mash the sweet potatoes for this recipe, so you have two options. One is simply to add roasted sweet potatoes to the fermenter as outlined above. Another is to do a mini-mash with just the sweet potatoes. Roast and coarsely mash them with a potato masher, then steep them in a colander placed inside a pot. Remove the colander with the potatoes after half an hour and add the rest of your brewing water to get to 7 gallons. (When removing the potatoes, take care not to allow them to float into the liquid outside of the colander or else you should strain them before boiling.) Bring to a boil. Slowly stir in 2 pounds of Munich liquid malt extract and 4 pounds 6 ounces of Pilsner liquid malt extract and boil for 90 minutes. Follow the hop and other ingredient schedules as outlined in the recipe.

Sage-Lemon Balm Saison (page 28)

Put 4 ounces of crushed Special B into a grain bag to steep in 7 gallons of water. Raise the temperature to 170 degrees Fahrenheit in about half an hour (if it comes to 170 more quickly, turn off heat and allow grains to steep for half an hour). Remove the grain bag and bring to a boil. Slowly stir in 6 pounds 11 ounces of Pilsner liquid malt extract and 10 ounces of cane sugar and boil for 90 minutes. Follow the hop and other ingredient schedules as outlined in the recipe.

Maple Porter (page 39)

Put 1 pound of crystal 80°L and 1 pound 4 ounces of chocolate malt into a grain bag to steep in 7 gallons of maple sap. Raise the temperature to 170 degrees Fahrenheit in about half an hour (if it comes to 170 more quickly, turn off heat and allow grains to steep for half an hour). Remove grain bag and bring to a boil. Slowly stir in 9 pounds of amber liquid malt extract and boil for 90 minutes. Follow the hop and other ingredient schedules as outlined in the recipe.

Dandelion Tonic (page 43)

Fill a kettle with 7 gallons of water. Bring water to a boil and slowly stir in 7 pounds of Pilsner liquid malt extract and 1 pound of amber liquid malt extract. Boil for 90 minutes. Follow the other ingredient schedules as outlined in the recipe.

Roasted Dandelion Root Stout (page 44)

Put 1 pound of roasted barley, 1 pound of Victory, 12 ounces of Special B, 8 ounces of chocolate malt, and 7 ounces of Carafoam into a grain bag to steep in 6½ gallons of water. Raise the temperature to 170 degrees Fahrenheit in about half an hour (if it comes to 170 more quickly, turn off heat and allow grains to steep for half an hour). Remove grain bag and bring to a boil. Slowly stir in 9 pounds 12 ounces of pale liquid malt extract and boil for 60 minutes. Follow the hop and other ingredient schedules as outlined in the recipe.

Spring Tonic (page 48)

Fill a kettle with 7 gallons of water. Bring to a boil and slowly stir in 6½ pounds of pale liquid malt extract. Boil for 90 minutes. Follow the other ingredient schedules as outlined in the recipe.

Nettle-Spicebush Ale (page 48)

Put 6 ounces of crushed crystal 80°L into a grain bag to steep in 6½ gallons of water. Raise the temperature to 170 degrees Fahrenheit in about half an hour (if it comes to 170 more quickly, turn off heat and allow grains to steep for half an hour). Remove grain bag and bring to a boil. Slowly stir in 7 pounds 4 ounces of pale liquid malt extract and boil for 90 minutes. Follow the hop and other ingredient schedules as outlined in the recipe.

Honeysuckle Blonde (page 53)

Put 10 ounces of crushed crystal 10°L and 6 ounces Special B into a grain bag to steep in 7 gallons of water. Raise the temperature to 170 degrees Fahrenheit in about half an hour (if it comes to 170 more quickly, turn off heat and allow grains to steep for half an hour). Remove grain bag and bring to a boil. Slowly stir in 7 pounds of pale liquid malt extract and boil for 90 minutes. Follow the hop and other ingredient schedules as outlined in the recipe.

Arugula Rye Porter (page 56)

Put 1 pound 2 ounces of crystal 80°L, 1 pound of chocolate malt, and 8 ounces of flaked wheat into a grain bag to steep in 6½ gallons of water. Raise the temperature to 170 degrees Fahrenheit in about half an hour (if it comes to 170 more quickly, turn off heat and allow grains to steep for half an hour). Remove grain bag and bring to a boil. Slowly stir in 7 pounds of liquid rye malt extract and boil for 60 minutes. Follow the hop and other ingredient schedules as outlined in the recipe.

Rhubarb Saison (page 60)

Fill a kettle with 7 gallons of water. Bring to a boil and slowly stir in 6 pounds 10 ounces of Pilsner liquid malt extract. Boil for 90 minutes. Follow the hop and other ingredient schedules as outlined in the recipe.

Chocolate Mint Stout (page 65)

Put 12 ounces of crystal 80°L, 12 ounces of chocolate malt, 8 ounces of roasted barley, and 4 ounces of Special B into a grain bag to steep in 6½ gallons of water. Raise the temperature to 170 degrees Fahrenheit in about half an hour (if it comes to 170 more quickly, turn off heat and allow grains to steep for half an hour). Remove grain bag and bring to a boil. Slowly stir in 7 pounds of pale liquid malt extract and boil for 90 minutes. Follow the hop and other ingredient schedules as outlined in the recipe.

Mumm (page 66)

Put 8 ounces of crystal 60°L, 5 ounces of roasted barley, and 4 ounces of midnight wheat into a grain bag to steep in 6½ gallons of water. Raise the temperature to 170 degrees Fahrenheit in about half an hour (if it comes to 170 more quickly, turn off heat and allow grains to steep for half an hour). Remove grain bag and bring to a boil. Slowly stir in 7½ pounds of pale liquid malt extract and ½ pound of rye malt extract and boil for 60 minutes. Follow the hop and other ingredient schedules as outlined in the recipe.

Chanterelle Bière de Garde (page 73)

Put 11 ounces of crystal 20°L into a grain bag to steep in 7 gallons of water. Raise the temperature to 170 degrees Fahrenheit in about half an hour (if it comes to 170 more quickly, turn off heat and allow grains to steep for half an hour). Remove grain bag and bring to a boil. Slowly stir in 7 pounds 12 ounces of Pilsner liquid malt extract and 1 pound of amber liquid malt extract and boil for 90 minutes. Follow

the hop and other ingredient schedules as outlined in the recipe.

Black Trumpet Milk Stout (page 76)

Put 13 ounces of crystal 80°L, 13 ounces of chocolate malt, and 13 ounces of roasted barley into a grain bag to steep in 6½ gallons of water. Raise the temperature to 170 degrees Fahrenheit in about half an hour (if it comes to 170 more quickly, turn off heat and allow grains to steep for half an hour). Remove grain bag and bring to a boil. Slowly stir in 5 pounds of pale liquid malt extract and 1 pound of amber liquid malt extract and boil for 60 minutes. Follow the hop and other ingredient schedules as outlined in the recipe.

Elderflower Witbier (page 80)

Fill kettle with 7 gallons of water. Bring to a boil. Slowly stir in 3 pounds 5 ounces of Pilsner liquid malt extract and 3 pounds 5 ounces of wheat liquid malt extract and boil for 90 minutes. Follow the hop and other ingredient schedules as outlined in the recipe.

Ebulon (page 83)

Fill kettle with 8 gallons of water. Bring to a boil. Slowly stir in 13 pounds of pale liquid malt extract and 1 pound of table sugar and boil for 120 minutes. Follow the hop and other ingredient schedules as outlined in the recipe.

Ginger-Spicebush Saison (page 86)

Put 13 ounces of crystal 80°L and 8 ounces of Special B into a grain bag to steep in 7 gallons of water. Raise the temperature to 170 degrees Fahrenheit in about half an hour (if it comes to 170 more quickly, turn off heat and allow grains to steep for half an hour). Remove grain bag and bring to a boil. Slowly stir in 8 pounds of pale liquid malt extract and boil for 90 minutes. Follow the hop and other ingredient schedules as outlined in the recipe.

Single Tree: Spicebush (page 89)
Put 10 ounces of Special B into a grain bag to steep in 7 gallons of water. Raise the temperature to 170 degrees Fahrenheit in about half an hour (if it comes to 170 more quickly, turn off heat and allow grains to steep for half an hour). Remove grain bag and bring to a boil. Slowly stir in 6 pounds of pale liquid malt extract and 1 pound of amber liquid malt extract and boil for 90 minutes. Follow the hop and other ingredient schedules as outlined in the recipe.

Sumac Saison (page 93)
Fill kettle with 7 gallons of water. Bring to a boil. Slowly stir in 6 pounds 10 ounces of Pilsner liquid malt extract and boil for 90 minutes. Follow the hop and other ingredient schedules as outlined in the recipe.

Sweet Clover Ale (page 95)
Put 10 ounces of crystal 60°L into a grain bag to steep in 6½ gallons of water. Raise the temperature to 170 degrees Fahrenheit in about half an hour (if it comes to 170 more quickly, turn off heat and allow grains to steep for half an hour). Remove grain bag and bring to a boil. Slowly stir in 7½ pounds of pale liquid malt extract and boil for 60 minutes. Follow the hop and other ingredient schedules as outlined in the recipe.

Basil Ale (page 98)
Put 6 ounces of crystal 60°L into a grain bag to steep in 6½ gallons of water. Raise the temperature to 170 degrees Fahrenheit in about half an hour (if it comes to 170 more quickly, turn off heat and allow grains to steep for half an hour). Remove grain bag

and bring to a boil. Slowly stir in 7 pounds of pale liquid malt extract and ½ pound of rye malt extract and boil for 60 minutes. Follow the hop and other ingredient schedules as outlined in the recipe.

Licorice Basil Schwarzbier (page 99)
Put 18 ounces of black malt and 4 ounces of chocolate malt into a grain bag to steep in 6½ gallons of water. Raise the temperature to 170 degrees Fahrenheit in about half an hour (if it comes to 170 more quickly, turn off heat and allow grains to steep for half an hour). Remove grain bag and bring to a boil. Slowly stir in 5 pounds 6 ounces of Pilsner liquid malt extract and 1 pound 4 ounces of amber liquid malt extract and boil for 90 minutes. Follow the hop and other ingredient schedules as outlined in the recipe.

Carrot-Ginger Saison (page 102)
Put 4 ounces of Special B into a grain bag to steep in 7 gallons of water. Raise the temperature to 170 degrees Fahrenheit in about half an hour (if it comes to 170 more quickly, turn off heat and allow grains to steep for half an hour). Remove grain bag and bring to a boil. Slowly stir in 7 pounds of Pilsner liquid malt extract and 1 pound of amber liquid malt extract and boil for 90 minutes. Follow the hop and other ingredient schedules as outlined in the recipe.

Carrot Seed Ale (page 105)
Fill kettle with 6½ gallons water. Bring to a boil. Slowly stir in 7 pounds 6 ounces of pale liquid malt extract and boil for 60 minutes. Follow the hop and other ingredient schedules as outlined in the recipe.

Sun-Dried Cherry Tomato Dark Strong (page 110)
Put 1 pound 4 ounces of Special B and 7 ounces of aromatic malt into a grain bag to steep in 7 gallons of water. Raise the temperature to 170 degrees

Fahrenheit in about half an hour (if it comes to 170 more quickly, turn off heat and allow grains to steep for half an hour). Remove grain bag and bring to a boil. Slowly stir in 9 pounds 10 ounces of Pilsner liquid malt extract and 1 pound 12 ounces of amber liquid malt extract and boil for 90 minutes. Follow the hop and other ingredient schedules as outlined in the recipe.

Green Tomato Saison (page 113)

Fill kettle with 7 gallons of water. Bring to a boil. Slowly stir in 7 pounds 5 ounces of Pilsner liquid malt extract and boil for 90 minutes. Follow the hop and other ingredient schedules as outlined in the recipe.

Belgian Fennel Stout (page 116)

Put 1 pound of chocolate malt, 12 ounces of 80°L, 4 ounces of Special B, and 4 ounces of roasted barley into a grain bag to steep in 6½ gallons of water. Raise the temperature to 170 degrees Fahrenheit in about half an hour (if it comes to 170 more quickly, turn off heat and allow grains to steep for half an hour). Remove grain bag and bring to a boil. Slowly stir in 8 pounds 6 ounces of pale liquid malt extract and boil for 60 minutes. Follow the hop and other ingredient schedules as outlined in the recipe.

Il Fortino (page 121)

Put 12 ounces of black malt, 10 ounces of chocolate malt, 1 pound of Carafoam, 4 ounces of Special B, and 4 ounces of roasted barley into a grain bag to steep in 6½ gallons of water. Raise the temperature to 170 degrees Fahrenheit in about half an hour (if it comes to 170 more quickly, turn off heat and allow grains to steep for half an hour). Remove grain bag and bring to a boil. Slowly stir in 9 pounds 10 ounces of pale liquid malt extract and boil for 60 minutes. Follow the hop and other ingredient schedules as outlined in the recipe.

Lavender Tripel (page 122)

Put 1 pound of Carafoam into a grain bag to steep in 7 gallons of water. Raise the temperature to 170 degrees Fahrenheit in about half an hour (if it comes to 170 more quickly, turn off heat and allow grains to steep for half an hour). Remove grain bag and bring to a boil. Slowly stir in 8 pounds of Pilsner liquid malt extract and 2 pounds of cane sugar and boil for 90 minutes. Follow the hop and other ingredient schedules as outlined in the recipe.

Peach Oak Abbey (page 126)

Put 10 ounces of Special B into a grain bag to steep in 7 gallons of water. Raise the temperature to 170 degrees Fahrenheit in about half an hour (if it comes to 170 more quickly, turn off heat and allow grains to steep for half an hour). Remove grain bag and bring to a boil. Slowly stir in 7½ pounds of Pilsner liquid malt extract and 1 pound of cane sugar and boil for 90 minutes. Follow the hop and other ingredient schedules as outlined in the recipe.

Gooseberry Golden (page 130)

Put 12 ounces of crystal 40°L into a grain bag to steep in 7 gallons of water. Raise the temperature to 170 degrees Fahrenheit in about half an hour (if it comes to 170 more quickly, turn off heat and allow grains to steep for half an hour). Remove grain bag and bring to a boil. Slowly stir in 7 pounds of Pilsner liquid malt extract and 1½ pounds of pale liquid malt extract and boil for 90 minutes. Follow the hop and other ingredient schedules as outlined in the recipe.

Paw Paw Abbey (page 134)

Put 1 pound of Carafoam, 8 ounces of Special B, and 4 ounces of crystal 40°L into a grain bag to steep in 7 gallons of water. Raise the temperature to 170 degrees Fahrenheit in about half an hour (if it comes to 170 more quickly, turn off heat and allow grains to steep for half an hour). Remove grain bag and bring to a boil. Slowly stir in 7 pounds 4 ounces of Pilsner liquid malt extract and 1 pound 4 ounces of wheat liquid malt extract and boil for 90 minutes. Follow the hop and other ingredient schedules as outlined in the recipe.

Pignut (page 142)

Fill a kettle with 7 gallons of water. Bring to a boil. Slowly stir in 8½ pounds of Pilsner liquid malt extract and boil for 90 minutes. Follow the hop and other ingredient schedules as outlined in the recipe.

Shagbark 80 Shilling (page 145)

Put 1 pound of crystal 20°L, 5 ounces of Special B, 4 ounces of crystal 40°L, and ½ ounce of chocolate malt into a grain bag to steep in 6½ gallons of water. Raise the temperature to 170 degrees Fahrenheit in about half an hour (if it comes to 170 more quickly, turn off heat and allow grains to steep for half an hour). Remove grain bag and bring to a boil. Slowly stir in 6½ pounds of pale liquid malt extract and boil for 60 minutes. Follow the hop and other ingredient schedules as outlined in the recipe.

Lotus Seed Bière de Garde (page 148)

Put 7 ounces of crystal 60°L, 7 ounces of pale chocolate malt, and 3 ounces of Special B into a grain bag to steep in 7 gallons of water. Raise the temperature to 170 degrees Fahrenheit in about half an hour (if it comes to 170 more quickly, turn off heat and allow grains to steep for half an hour). Remove grain bag and bring to a boil. Slowly stir in 8 pounds 12 ounces of amber liquid malt extract and boil for 90 minutes. Follow the hop and other ingredient schedules as outlined in the recipe.

Single Tree: Oak (page 154)

Put 10 ounces of crystal 30°L, 5 ounces of crystal 40°L, 5 ounces of crystal 60°L, and 3 ounces of black malt into a grain bag to steep in 6½ gallons of water. Raise the temperature to 170 degrees Fahrenheit in about half an hour (if it comes to 170 more quickly, turn off heat and allow grains to steep for half an hour). Remove grain bag and bring to a boil. Slowly stir in 7 pounds of amber liquid malt extract and boil for 60 minutes. Follow the hop and other ingredient schedules as outlined in the recipe.

Persimmon-Spicebush Bière de Garde (page 158)

Put 4 ounces of Special B into a grain bag to steep in 7 gallons of water. Raise the temperature to 170 degrees Fahrenheit in about half an hour (if it comes to 170 more quickly, turn off heat and allow grains to steep for half an hour). Remove grain bag and bring to a boil. Slowly stir in 8 pounds 12 ounces of pale liquid malt extract and 4 ounces of table sugar and boil for 90 minutes. Follow the hop and other ingredient schedules as outlined in the recipe.

Smoked Apple Ale (page 163)

Put 8 ounces of German smoked malt into a grain bag to steep in 6½ gallons of water. Raise the temperature to 170 degrees Fahrenheit in about half an hour (if it comes to 170 more quickly, turn off heat and allow grains to steep for half an hour). Remove grain bag and bring to a boil. Slowly stir in 5 pounds 12 ounces of pale liquid malt extract and 1½ pounds of wheat liquid malt extract and boil for 60 minutes. Follow the hop and other ingredient schedules as outlined in the recipe.

Sour Apple (page 164)

Fill a kettle with 6½ gallons of water. Bring to a boil. Slowly stir in 6 pounds 10 ounces of Pilsner liquid malt extract and 14 ounces of amber liquid malt extract and boil for 90 minutes. Follow the hop and other ingredient schedules as outlined in the recipe.

Sassquash (page 168)

Fill a kettle with 7 gallons of water. Bring to a boil. Slowly stir in 5 pounds of pale liquid malt extract and 2½ pounds of Pilsner liquid malt extract and boil for 90 minutes. Follow the hop and other ingredient schedules as outlined in the recipe.

Pumpkin Seed Ale (page 171)

Fill a kettle with 6½ gallons of water. Bring to a boil. Slowly stir in 7 pounds of pale liquid malt extract and boil for 60 minutes. Follow the hop and other ingredient schedules as outlined in the recipe.

Horseradish Stout (page 174)

Put 1 pound of chocolate malt, 12 ounces of crystal 80°L, 8 ounces of roasted barley, and 6 ounces of Special B into a grain bag to steep in 6½ gallons of water. Raise the temperature to 170 degrees Fahrenheit in about half an hour (if it comes to 170 more quickly, turn off heat and allow grains to steep for half an hour). Remove grain bag and bring to a boil. Slowly stir in 8 pounds of amber liquid malt extract and ½ pound of rye malt extract and boil for 60 minutes. Follow the hop and other ingredient schedules as outlined in the recipe.

Burdock Rauchbier (page 178)

Put 12 ounces of crystal 40°L, 4 ounces of chocolate malt, and 1½ pounds of German smoked malt into a grain bag to steep in 6½ gallons of water. Raise the temperature to 170 degrees Fahrenheit in about half an hour (if it comes to 170 more quickly, turn off heat and allow grains to steep for half an hour). Remove grain bag and bring to a boil. Slowly stir in 7 pounds of amber liquid malt extract and boil for 60 minutes. Follow the hop and other ingredient schedules as outlined in the recipe.

Ginger Beer (page 182)

Fill a kettle with 6½ gallons of water. Bring to a boil. Slowly stir in 5 pounds of pale liquid malt extract and boil for 60 minutes. Follow the hop and other ingredient schedules as outlined in the recipe.

Winter Warmer (page 185)

Put 8 ounces of crystal 80°L, 8 ounces of chocolate, and 4 ounces of Special B into a grain bag to steep in 6½ gallons of water. Raise the temperature to 170 degrees Fahrenheit in about half an hour (if it comes to 170 more quickly, turn off heat and allow grains to steep for half an hour). Remove grain bag and bring to a boil. Slowly stir in 9 pounds of Munich liquid malt extract and boil for 60 minutes. Follow the hop and other ingredient schedules as outlined in the recipe.

Turmeric Tripel (page 190)

Fill a kettle with 7 gallons of water. Bring to a boil. Slowly stir in 11½ pounds of Pilsner liquid malt extract and 1 pound 12 ounces of table sugar and boil for 90 minutes. Follow the hop and other ingredient schedules as outlined in the recipe.

INDEX

V

Velcro, 176

W

Washington, Martha, 128
water mint, 62
weis beers, 19, 128, 133, 164

Weisenbock, 133

Weisenbock, 133
whirlfloc, xxxi
wild cherry, xxiii, 32
Wild Grapevine Wee Heavy, 17, 195
Winter Warmer, 185, 201
witbier, 19, 80, 84, 128
wormwood, xxix, 26, 118
wort, xvi

Y

yams, 22, 166
yeast, xvi, 15, 108, 161. See also Saccharomyces